Nature
is all that
we see,
all that
we want,
all that
we love.

George Sand, 'À Aurore', 1873

Design for a hellebore corsage brooch, Joseph Chaumet,
drawing studio, c. 1890, gouache and wash on translucent paper.

CHAUMET
DRAWING FROM NATURE

Gaëlle Rio

Botanical texts: Marc Jeanson

Design for a carnation corsage brooch, Joseph Chaumet, drawing studio,
c. 1890, gouache and wash on translucent paper.

Preface

The act of drawing predates all other kinds of artistic creation and is thus their ancestor. High Jewellery is no exception, since producing a drawing is the first step in a jeweller's creative process: it expresses the original intention of the designer and, like a musical score, serves as a technical guide as to how it should be made. Although a drawing of this kind is destined to be overshadowed by the beauty and sumptuousness of the end result, it is nevertheless an object that gives aesthetic pleasure in its own right. The language of drawing strips a piece of jewellery down to its essentials, as well as providing a wonderful record that forms part of the legacy of a jeweller.

Chaumet's creative spirit and stylistic nuances are laid bare in tens of thousands of sketches and preparatory drawings in pencil or gouache. This body of work miraculously mixes lightness and power, motion and stillness, presence and discretion. Our senses are dazzled by the bold delicacy – or the refined audacity – that distinguishes Chaumet from the other Maisons.

The theme of nature runs all the way through the array of motifs explored in these drawings. Chaumet himself was not only a virtuoso jeweller, but also an attentive observer who depicted the natural world in detail. To the traditional forms of snakes and butterflies were added ants and maybugs, while classic roses were joined by reeds, ferns and ivy. This fascinating use of plants and animals at Chaumet mirrors current concerns. Apart from the pleasing visual effect of these motifs taken straight from nature (both domesticated and wild), the drawings call into question our relationship with the world around us. In an era marked by a spectacular profusion of images, the simplicity of line and economical use of colour on these sheets of paper are a legacy of distant times, revealing Chaumet's long-standing love of fauna and flora as well as the singularity of nature at its most intimate. The discovery and examination of these designs today provide a salutary lesson in both understanding the living world and delving into the creative process. Once a piece of jewellery has been made, sold and worn, the original drawing represents – in all its purity and sincerity – an enduring connection with the timeless beauty of nature and thus acquires the status of a work of art.

The Art
of
Drawing
Jewellery

THE ORIGINS OF A JEWEL

Drawing was once considered to be above all a learning exercise, a tool for research or a way of producing preparatory studies, but it gradually grew in status during the 19th century and was finally recognised as an art form in its own right. Pablo Picasso stated that 'drawing is no joke. … Obviously, you never know what you are going to draw … but once you start, a story or an idea appears … and there you are! Then the story gets bigger, as in the theatre, as in life … and the drawing turns into other drawings, into a veritable novel.'[1] The real power of drawing lies in its expression of an initial idea or of the creative impulse, its incarnation of the artist's intentions and its capacity to convey them. Drawings of jewellery were first exhibited only recently, and they have barely been studied, and rarely published. They have long occupied a humble position in the hierarchy of the arts because they serve a technical purpose, but also on account of the status of jewellery itself. Jewels occupy an unusual place in art history because, leaving aside any consideration of them as objets d'art, they are above all fashion accessories with a specific purpose, displayed as required and subjected to any number of configurations and transformations. A jewel is made to be worn and thus reflects the taste of its owner, who lives within a particular society and in a specific era.

Until the 19th century, observers viewed jewellery as a minor art form since it was made by a whole chain of artisans, from modellers to polishers,[2] rather than by an individual artist conceiving his or her work on an intellectual level. According to the rules of craftsmanship, a drawing of a piece of jewellery serves as a reference and guide for all the 'hands' involved in the creation of the jewel. Since the Renaissance, sketching a jewel has represented the first visible step in the process of creation, giving life to an idea and enabling it to be turned into reality. This process was advocated by the jeweller Augustin Duflos back in the 18th century: 'Before practising his art, a jeweller must therefore be ready to study drawing on a regular basis,' he wrote.[3] Realising an idea through drawing is a sign of the sophistication of the historical manufacturing process. Drawing is still used systematically in top-end jewellery, 'but it has always been the first and primordial stage in the creation of jewellery,' writes the historian Michaël Decrossas. 'There are undoubtedly several historical and practical reasons for this. The most decisive is the fact that, until the turn of the 16th century, Parisian jewellers merely had to make mounts for stones that had already been cut by other artisans. The jewellery drawing surely had its origins here, as an inventive starting point that mapped out the assemblage and combination of stones while also highlighting them through the mount. This enduring principle gave drawing its first specificity: it is always, at level 1, that of the stones and, therefore, the mount.'[4] Such drawings, made to scale and often in colour (in order to distinguish between the stones and the mount), used shading or white highlights to give the impression of relief and guided artisans through the piece's manufacturing process. A drawing not only provides information about this process (while also reflecting the tastes of the customer and the supplier), but also stands as the only record of a jewel once it has been sold and has disappeared into the hands of its new owner. Thus, despite the drawing's primary function as a technical tool, it also acquires an aesthetic value, which is further enhanced by its value as a heritage item. A jewellery drawing can therefore be viewed as a veritable work of art that touches us through its beauty and its history.

Opposite, above
Design for a bee brooch,
Chaumet, drawing studio, c. 1970,
graphite pencil and gouache
on tracing paper.

Opposite, below
Design for a pig brooch,
Chaumet, drawing studio, c. 1970,
graphite pencil and gouache
on tracing paper.

This twin focus – aesthetic and historical – underlies our examination of the exceptional body of artistic work, comprising 66,000 drawings, produced in the last two and a half centuries by jewellers from Maison Chaumet, 'one of the doyennes of the Parisian luxury industry',[5] as a prelude to the creation of their precious jewels. The majority of these sheets are conserved in albums that were compiled in the 19th century, each dedicated to a different type of jewellery: tiaras, brooches, stomachers, aigrettes ... Although very few are dated (as is often the case with preparatory studies and technical sketches), most of them were executed in the 19th century, but there is also a particularly substantial series preserved from the years 1890 to 1930. Over and above any chronological considerations, the most notable feature here is the diversity of the media involved – pencil, watercolour, ink and gouache – and the great variety of approaches. There are initial sketches (which best reflect the jeweller's creative spark), working drawings on tracing paper, and gouaches whose artistic qualities were intended to win over potential customers. All in all, 'they form, in a sense, an archaeological record of the jewels in Chaumet's history'.[6] This astonishingly rich and abundant collection, embracing masterpieces and preliminary studies, finished drawings and repeated motifs, was built up over the course of time, without foresight, and was consolidated as a legacy over the course of the 19th century.

FROM INSPIRATION TO PRODUCTION, FROM LINE TO FORM

Everything starts in the drawing studio. The first step in the process of creating a jewel, a finished jewellery drawing is itself often the end result of considerable work involving a great number of sketches. The person responsible for the drawing is thus the first to bring a piece of jewellery to life, having followed the instructions of the artistic director. Their hand is guided by experience and inspiration, but also by their knowledge of the specific characteristics of a particular jewel and the technical constraints that might affect the final outcome. Their imagination is circumscribed by their understanding of the possibilities and limitations of the materials featured in their drawing.

Such drawings convey a personal vision of a particular project while also reflecting the identity and creative world of Maison Chaumet itself. A jewellery drawing starts with a few ideas jotted down in black pencil or graphite in a sketchbook, without the artist necessarily having a jewel in mind at this point. This first phase is distinguished by free-flowing lines that bear witness to the designer's inspiration. Out of these numerous ideas, maybe only one will be selected to be reworked, improved and shaped into a specific type of jewel that takes into account the choice of stones and other materials. If the resulting design is chosen for production, a full-scale version is then traced onto thin paper, to serve as a model for the workshop. The transparency of tracing paper (first introduced in the second half of the 19th century) highlights certain sections of the drawing through the play of light. These drawings may be executed in pen or pencil, although they are mainly filled in with watercolour, and they show in great detail the technical approach that should be followed during manufacture. They sometimes even include precise descriptions of the materials involved, as well as the amount of stones required and their exact weights. Drawings such as these exerted a decisive influence over the customer, who would peruse a simple sketch or a complete watercolour before commissioning a piece. Accordingly, there are

Top Design for a laurel-branch tiara,
Joseph Chaumet, drawing studio, 1900–10,
gouache and wash on tinted paper.

Above Design for a laurel-leaf tiara,
Joseph Chaumet, drawing studio, 1910, gouache,
wash and gold pigment on tinted paper.

often several different designs of the same piece of jewellery in the archives, dozens having been discarded prior to the definitive order. In 1852, in a letter addressed to Jules Fossin, the Maison's director, the Russian prince and artistic patron Anatoly Demidov mentioned 'the pencil drawings' that he had been shown for gemstone mosaics that would adorn snuffboxes, and requested a 'coloured drawing' for the next stage of 'the project submitted [to him], which seemed very attractive'. In the late 19th century, Édouard Wibaille, Chaumet's master draughtsman from 1886 to 1903, began to produce a huge number of different versions of a single motif in his quest for perfection, although he limited himself to recording the jewel's lines and form, leaving its colours to the imagination.

Once a drawing was approved by the artistic director, the colours were added, to initiate a second, more complete phase in the design process. A single object was represented on the page, its contours now more fully defined and its materials more recognisable, with stones appropriately cut and coloured. Following the tradition of nature artists, Chaumet's draughtsmen were fond of gouache and watercolour, whose colours resembled those of the natural world and which possessed an unrivalled capacity to reflect the brilliance and subtle tones of precious gemstones and pearls. Furthermore, they allowed for drawings to be reworked and corrected if necessary. The colouring process brought out all the Oriental allure of fine pearls and the dazzle of precious stones, gold and platinum. Facetted diamonds were depicted with thick layers of white gouache, while bodycolour was employed for other precious stones. The final stage in the drawing process took the form of a life-size gouache, made with fine brushstrokes on coloured paper, that accentuated the contrasts between the different elements that made up the piece. This technically demanding exercise served not only to record a jewel's size but also to capture the materials used and to convey an illusion of relief: a two-dimensional drawing had to evoke a three-dimensional object. The colours worked in conjunction with the lighting (which traditionally came from the upper left corner of the drawing) to reproduce the tones and shapes of the gemstones as convincingly as possible. A piece of jewellery was often drawn from several angles, and sometimes a supplementary drawing was added to show it being worn or to reveal parts that were hidden from view.

These drawings served as guides for the various artisans who together brought the designs to life: modellers, cutters, gemologists and setters. A jeweller would use these studies to assess the feasibility of a project, while an expert gemologist would take note of the stones involved. As the art historian Guillaume Glorieux has pointed out, 'The gouache would serve as a reference for all the participants in the production of a jewel, as well as constituting a work of art in its own right.'[7] These superb gouaches, sometimes called 'presentation drawings',[8] went beyond merely providing customers with a pre-production proposal, also preserving its poetic memory. The gouaches that formed the basis of sumptuous imperial commissions from 1805 to 1811, such as Charlemagne's crown and Napoléon's Gladius sword, constitute one of the most remarkable collections in the annals of jewellery. Although gouaches are still produced today, honouring the tradition established during Chaumet's illustrious history, they are now based on photographs of a finished piece. Nevertheless, the gouaches made for the contemporary collection entitled *Les Ciels de Chaumet* follow the same creative protocol and artistic route as their predecessors. The original role of a drawing, as a technical and aesthetic guide to the production of a jewel after a customer's go-ahead, has been superseded: it now serves as an illustration for advertising and press campaigns, accompanying new sales and communications strategies. In any case, once a jewel has been created and thus converted into a heritage item, its corresponding gouache enters into the Maison's archives and becomes a powerful record. These colour drawings are sometimes complemented by additional illustrations showing a jewel being worn on the body, revealing how jewellery can be enhanced and given a new lease of life, and how certain components can be removed to divide and transform one piece into several different items.

Jewellery design goes beyond line and colour, however, to encompass form and volume. A sketch has to be turned into a three-dimensional object. According to Jean-Auguste-Dominique Ingres, that great advocate of the primacy of drawing over colour, 'Drawing is not merely a matter of reproducing contours; a drawing does not simply consist of lines: it is also expression, inner form, the plan, the model.'[9] The Maison's jeweller Jean-Baptiste Fossin and his son Jules (both sculptors who exhibited at the Salon) produced drawings resembling sculptures on paper, working on the design and the materials in tandem and inventing new techniques, such as one method (which they patented) for encrusting fine gemstones with gold thread. From then on, sculpting jewels and dreaming up jewel sculptures became a tradition at the Maison. The gold pieces designed around 1850 by Jean-Valentin Morel, for example, are nothing short of miniature monuments. Joseph Chaumet subsequently included an additional step in his creative process, producing *maillechort* models [10] after the drawings, akin to a sculptor's plaster casts or an architect's maquettes: 'What surprising variety, what fantasies can be found in the forms of these ornaments and their decoration! Some are complicated like elaborate lacework, while others are reduced almost to a simple metal circle set off by a few stones. What differences in style, too, from old-style First Empire tiaras with simple arched lines, albeit loaded with the gemstones typical of the modern artist, to those huge ornaments recalling the national Kokoshnick of Russia, intended for the Grand Duchesses of the Romanov family!'[11]

This final stage before a jewel is manufactured transforms a drawing into a three-dimensional object. Models were used mainly for pieces intended to be worn on the head. Once they had been cut out and shaped, they were embellished with gouache (to show the colour of the selected stones) and sometimes even gum arabic (to simulate their sparkle). A customer could thus try on her future tiara and make any last-minute adjustments; without the distraction of real diamonds or gemstones, the elegance of the outline was fundamental. Nickel-silver models reached their peak in the period between 1880 and 1930, but they are still made today and dispatched to customers for inspection and approval. Otherwise, more mundane approximations of jewels are produced in plaster or plasticine after the gouache, resulting in an actual-size preview that gives an accurate impression of an item's volume and thickness. Modifications can then be made with wax. A modeller works in close collaboration with the studio designer, using tools similar to those of a jeweller but with different materials, including rhinestones and tin. For practical reasons, a model is often an assemblage of various components. It provides an opportunity to anticipate possible technical problems that are not apparent in a drawing, and it also allows a jewel's ergonomics, flexibility and comfort to be put to the test. Once it is finished, a model serves as a life-size reference for the production phase.

For thirty years, jewellery drawings have experienced a sea change: they can now be constructed directly in three dimensions on a computer. Pencils have been replaced by software, and sheets of paper by a screen, marking a return to purely technical drawing. It is now possible to make 3-D simulations of jewellery with a previously unimaginable degree of detail, including specifications of thickness, weight and wearability, before moving on to manufacture. But the resulting image appears, paradoxically, devoid of relief and texture, now that it is deprived of the aesthetic freedom that derived from pencil drawing. For all its undoubted advantages for jewellery production, this technical advance has therefore failed to eliminate the hand-drawing phase that is still so beloved by Maison Chaumet. The house's current graphic output is thus the result of a successful alliance between tastes forged by a historical legacy and the digital techniques intrinsic to contemporary jewellery.

FROM THE DRAWING STUDIO TO THE WORKSHOP: ARTISTIC VIRTUOSOS

'It goes without saying that a company like this does not imitate, it does not copy anything, and it can sign each and every one of its creations, just as painters sign their works. Artists of proven talent are thus attached to a department of studies and drawing, or to another department of modelling and sculpture, with responsibility for clarifying details and fine-tuning a design for production, in the light of pre-established technical requirements.'[12] According to the journalist and art critic Gustave Babin, Maison Chaumet is an artistic institution more than a jewellery workshop, despite the misplaced labelling of jewellery as a minor art form under the banner of 'decorative arts'. The creative process at Chaumet is distinguished by the involvement right from the start of graphic artists and painters endowed with the enormous privilege of providing a stylistic direction by conjuring up subjects, outlining mounts and establishing colour ranges. If we go right back to the Maison's earliest days, its founder, Marie-Étienne Nitot (1750–1809), trained at the Royal Free School of Art in Paris[13] before becoming official jeweller to the imperial court in 1805. The painter Jean-Baptiste Fossin (1786–1848) also studied at an art school and was described as a gifted draughtsman by the renowned jeweller and collector Henri Vever: '[He] draws as easily as he speaks. He is a virtuoso with a pencil who makes light of drawing, chatting all the while with an awestruck customer overwhelmed by his charming improvisations.'[14] In 1889, when the visionary Joseph Chaumet (1852–1928) took over the Maison (and put his name to it), he established a genuine drawing and sculpture studio, with its own manager and a full-time staff of several acclaimed draughtsmen. Their employment contracts specified that they thereby made a 'formal commitment not to work for any other company, even outside working hours'.[15]

During the Belle Époque, Édouard Wibaille, the head of the drawing studio, was responsible for the Maison's artistic policy. Accordingly, in 1899 he published a 'Report addressed to Monsieur Chaumet about the various phases through which jewellery and goldsmithing have passed in the last few years and the advantages that these could occasion, an inventory of the developments that followed the successful emergence of the Art Nouveau style'. Wibaille

Top Design for a butterfly brooch that can
be converted into an aigrette, Joseph Chaumet,
drawing studio, 1900, graphite pencil, gouache
and wash on tinted paper.

Above Design for a butterfly brooch that
can be converted into an aigrette, Joseph Chaumet,
drawing studio, c. 1910, graphite pencil, gouache
and wash on tinted paper.

15

detected a new-found hunger for innovation within the Maison: 'Everything that seemed audacious – excessively so – just a few years ago seems perfectly natural for us today.'[16] He was awarded a gold medal to mark the 1900 Universal Exposition in Paris,[17] in recognition of his extraordinary imagination, devoted to capturing jewels on paper. An examination of his drawings helps us understand that a magnificent jewel is, above all else, a beautiful design. Henri Delaspre succeeded Wibaille as head of the drawing and sculpture studio in the 1900s, and had five other draughtsmen working under him: Chamson, Denizot, Hauck, Morlet and Silvestri. The latter two were responsible for tracing the scale drawings that were passed on to the jewellers.[18] The draughtsmen numbered each drawing on the back, as well as adding their initials. These drawings were then collected in albums that were classified by type of jewellery: tiaras and bands, rings, bracelets, brooches and barrettes, earrings, etc. Each drawing was also listed by number in a separate book and accompanied by a description. Joseph Chaumet's son, Marcel, followed in his father's footsteps and similarly placed great importance on drawing. It was he who hired the enormously talented René Morin (1932–2017), who put new wind in the Maison's sails. His drawings conveyed his love of rough, bold materials and textures, undoubtedly nurtured by his early training as a sculptor.

These pioneers, working at the crossroads of art, fashion and technology, demonstrated an undoubted love of drawing, but their talents were reined in by certain conditions, as Babin was already pointing out in 1830. Their output was dependent 'either on subjects thought up by the management, sometimes in sketches or perfunctory indications, or on often vague proposals formulated by a customer'.[19] Chaumet's graphic artists did not sign their sketches or gouaches since their work was at the service of the team's collective vision. Their drawings may not be entirely anonymous, but ultimately they are solely attributable to Maison Chaumet. Apart from a few famous historical figures, the identity of these artisans remains largely obscure, although their choice of paper and colours, as well as their graphic style and composition, allow us to discern common elements and thus make out individual bodies of work.

If we go back to the times of Nitot, Fossin and Chaumet – or, more recently, to that of Pierre Sterlé – it is clear that Maison Chaumet has maintained a highly artistic approach to jewellery in which drawing has always played a central role. Even today, this graphic sensibility is a constant feature of the production process behind every new collection. A theme chosen by the creative director is illustrated by an array of images, with reference to the Maison icons (from oak-leaf tiaras to *Joséphine* rings) that are constantly re-examined. The creative studio sends a drawing of each piece due for production to the workshop, ushering in a new phase that involves a quest for the right stones by an expert gemologist and an interpretation of volume by the Maison's jewellers under the watchful eyes of the setters and polishers.

FROM ARTWORK TO HERITAGE: THE POWER OF DRAWING

Throughout Chaumet's long creative history (which itself reflects the history of France), an infinite succession of drawings – pendants, brooches, rings, necklaces, tiaras, earrings, pins and clips – have filled up entire albums, bearing witness to an unfailing virtuosity kept up from one generation to the next and distinguished by careful observation, exquisite lines and a profound understanding of materials. This exemplary graphic resource reveals the constant dialogue between tradition and innovation underlying the field of decorative art in general, manifested through an interplay between continuity and rupture, between quotations from the past and reinterpretations in the present, that constitutes a history of forms and tastes.

Aside from their unerring virtuosity, the creative power of Chaumet's drawings allows the Maison to embark on ventures that would otherwise be constrained by the cost of materials, since potential production problems are irrelevant to examples of purely graphic invention. The Maison's precious order books abound with demonstrations of daring and the extraordinary character and spirit that runs through its creations. These drawings are composed in a painterly fashion, with subtle shifts of balance that invert the volumes or the centre of gravity of a setting. As Fabienne Reybaud, an expert in luxury brands, has observed, 'Over and above the technical virtuosity, there is always a tension, a dynamic in the arrangement and association of plant forms. And, above all, the Maison manages to put a distance between the apparent humility of the subjects that are being treated – basic, accessible, familiar from nature – and the preciousness of objects made from platinum, gold and diamonds. As if by cultivating this kind of 'grandeur of simplicity', Chaumet had found its jewellery oxymoron.'[20]

Jewels are fragile: stones can fall off and enamel can crack, making jewellery one of the most ephemeral of all the arts. Furthermore, precious metals can arouse envy. Jewellery can also embody private stories on a personal or family level, but even when pieces are sold and worn, their corresponding drawings continue to belong to Chaumet. They represent a formidable archive of treasures that can often no longer be traced: 'If you want to build a monument that will last for ever, draw it on paper or build it in granite; if it is made of gold, its existence will be ephemeral as it is associated with the most costly metal known to mankind,' writes one historian.[21] The talent of its graphic artists and its long-term vision have meant that the Maison's jewellery drawings represent far more than a mere technical guide. By capturing the very first ideas behind a piece of jewellery, a drawing establishes itself as a work of art; by sometimes becoming the last vestige of the finished creation, it also serves as a heritage item. Moreover, the 'paper museum'[22] formed by this incredible collection of graphic art provides an inexhaustible resource for the drawing studio by forging links between the creativity of yesteryear and that of tomorrow.

Design for a leaf-motif tiara with diamonds and blue sapphires, Joseph Chaumet, drawing studio, c. 1900, gouache and wash on translucent paper.

Drawing from Nature

NATURE DRAWINGS

'Nature runs through the history of the arts, ephemeral and eternal, fragile and immortal, overriding all other sources of inspiration,' writes the jewellery specialist Alba Cappellieri.[1] The representation of nature is crucial to jewellery design, and it has been at the heart of Maison Chaumet's creative output right from the start. Around one-half of the firm's 66,000 drawings feature natural elements: coiled snakes, stars, feathers, clover leaves, palmettes and flowers of all kinds combine to reflect a nature that is bountiful, free and vibrant, but never idealised. As the journalist Fabienne Reybaud has stated, 'Nature is neither good nor bad at Chaumet: it just is.'[2] The company's designers have observed nature closely in order to depict it in all its diversity and authenticity, from the bees that represented the Empire to timeless symbols of ears of wheat (denoting prosperity) and the hortensias that evoked Joséphine (whose passion for these flowers led her to name her daughter Hortense). Nature can be wild and untamed, as in the monumental 15-piece epergne (table centrepiece)[3] that was delivered to the Polish prince Leon Radziwill in 1846, which shows a heron attacking a lizard under a cedar tree. In contrast, it can also be orderly and accessible, as in the quasi-scientific drawings of birds' heads and feet from the 1840s, and in the sketches of bulrushes, oats and wheat from the end of the 19th century. Nature can also be domesticated, as in the design for an ice bucket with two white bears making up the handles and hunters in a rocky landscape forming the main body of the piece. These accomplished renditions of different aspects of the natural world demonstrate artistic refinement applied to the discipline of scientific observation.

Over and above the iconography that borrowed from nature's motley array, these drawings are also distinguished by their aesthetic value. They are jewellery designs rather than botanical drawings, illustrating Chaumet's pictorial and sculptural vision – and, more broadly, the evolution of the Maison's imaginative approach over nearly two and a half centuries. Ever since 1780, when it was founded by Marie-Étienne Nitot, the Maison (which adopted the name of Chaumet in 1889) has always been a remarkable interpreter of its times. It has reflected prevailing artistic movements, resulting in the prolific creativity displayed throughout the 19th and 20th centuries. A perusal of these thousands of sheets of paper brings to life various approaches to the representation of nature that have been current since the 18th century, tracing a history that can be summarised – according to Alvar González-Palacios, a specialist in the decorative arts – in the dichotomy between the straight line and the curve: 'An alternation between the straight line and the curve seems to embody the history of styles very succinctly. There is an eternal interplay between restraint and emphasis, between peacefulness and passion, between abstraction and naturalism. Everything takes place within the conflict between geometry and botany.'[4] The attentive observation of nature in the 19th century gave way to an emphasis on stylisation, imbued with fantasy and imagination, in the 20th and 21st centuries.

NATURE AS AN EMBLEM OF IMPERIAL POWER

Ever since the beginnings of Maison Chaumet, nature has been at the heart of its creative practice. Having worked under Ange-Joseph Aubert (Queen

Opposite, above
Design for a butterfly brooch,
Joseph Chaumet, drawing
studio, c. 1900, graphite
pencil, gouache and wash
on tinted paper.

Opposite, below
Design for a beetle brooch,
Joseph Chaumet, drawing
studio, c. 1900, graphite
pencil, gouache and wash
on tinted paper.

Marie-Antoinette's jeweller), Marie-Étienne Nitot was commissioned, along with his son François-Regnault (1779–1853), to set the diamond known as 'the Regent' in Napoléon Bonaparte's consular sword. After setting jewels in one of the crowns used for Napoléon's coronation as Emperor in 1804 (inspired by Charlemagne's crown), the Nitots became official jewellers to the imperial court in 1805 and went on to create sumptuous pieces that reflected the Empire's pomp and power. Their jewellery was based on simple, symmetrical designs arranged around a central axis, decorated with motifs intended to evoke classical antiquity, such as palmettes, honeysuckle, oak twigs, olive and laurel leaves, vine garlands and acanthus scrolls. This style – at one and the same time austere and imposing, grandiose and timeless – is exemplified by a parure of oak leaves with cornelian etching created around 1809. The Nitots' designs also incorporated eagles and fleurs-de-lis, royal and imperial emblems that Napoléon borrowed from great civilisations of the past. This Neoclassical return to ancient forms and subjects found its echo in the pure lines and sharp contours perfected by the likes of Jacques-Louis David, Jean-Auguste-Dominique Ingres and Pierre-Paul Prud'hon. Natural motifs such as ears of wheat came back into fashion after the archaeological discovery of Herculaneum in 1713 and Pompeii in 1755 – and they also received, in their turn, the Nitots' stylised classical treatment.

The late 18th century witnessed great developments in botany, but the discipline also gave rise to a fashion that was imbued with a pre-Romantic visionary spirit. Marie-Étienne Nitot and the Empress Joséphine shared a passion for flowers and animals that could be indulged in the hothouse of the Château de Malmaison, a construction 50 metres (164 feet) long that was heated by coal-fired stoves. Here, rare birds could fly around freely, and an unmatched plant collection, grown from seeds imported from all over the world, could flourish. Joséphine had acquired a boundless enthusiasm for plants, and more particularly exotic species, during her childhood in Martinique. Indeed, 'the Empress had always loved flowers and had always gathered around her flowers or any other plant that attracted her attention. Her taste for plants thus grew to a greater degree as soon as she came into possession of land and a garden.'[5] Pierre-Joseph Redouté (1759–1840), 'Her Majesty's flower painter', drew inspiration from the 200 varieties of rose planted at Malmaison to create a beautiful series of hand-coloured illustrations entitled *Les Roses* (botanists acknowledged the Empress's patronage by naming one of these roses *Josephinia imperatricis*). Nitot, a devotee of art and art history, channelled this subject matter into his jewellery, and his approach to nature was echoed by his successors throughout the 19th century. Joséphine loved jewellery as much as she loved flowers, and her influence can be seen in the profusion of tiaras decorated with flowers and foliage that appear throughout the Maison's albums of drawings from the years following the Restoration (1814). She was ahead of her time, as she anticipated the boom in Romantic naturalism that would infuse the preparatory drawings for objets d'art and jewellery in the 1830s and 1840s.

In 1811, the Emperor commissioned a new series of crown jewels from François-Regnault Nitot. These were notable particularly for their 150 ears of wheat, which complemented the diamonds that he had prepared the previous year for the new Empress to wear on her bodice or in her hair. Joséphine's wheat-ear tiara was a prime example of Nitot's handling of natural motifs and perfectly encapsulated the Empire style in jewellery, with its 'verve of line, realism of movement that makes the ears look windswept, and the modernity of its design'.[6] In the words of the art historian Diana Scarisbrick, 'the imposing assortment of jewellery on tiaras, combs, earrings, brooches and bracelets, richly adorned with rare pearls and precious stones, transformed the bourgeois Bonapartes into kings and queens.'[7]

NATURE TRIUMPHANT IN THE 19TH CENTURY

This depiction of nature came into its own in the 19th century, initially as a demonstration of the power of the Empire and its emblems. During this time of industrial expansion and political upheavals, jewellery – which previously had been the exclusive preserve of royalty and the aristocracy – began to be worn by the bourgeoisie as well. This period also saw a boom in coloured drawings, which became recognised as works of art in their own right and provided the perfect vehicle for artists seeking a faithful transcription of the natural world. Although nature drawing was obviously not a 19th-century invention, it emerged as an effective tool for capturing natural features without idealising them or subjecting them to any personal artistic interpretation, in order to arrive at a representation that was as objective and accurate as possible. As the traveller, archivist and historian Francis Wey used to say, 'Only the true is beautiful,'[8] – and the designers at Chaumet accordingly devoted themselves to revealing the truth of nature.

The Romantic spirit

'In its springtime, Romanticism touched every branch of art and filled them all with a sap of renewal,' claimed the critic Gustave Babin.[9] During the Restoration and the July Monarchy (1830–48), this nature-loving movement gave fresh impetus to one of the favourite motifs of *ancien régime* jewellery and broke with the rigid Classicism of the Empire style. Jewellery now embodied a combination of elegance, lightness and naturalness, becoming more airy and less ostentatious. Bracelets were worn in pairs, and belts on dresses and headwear adorned with natural or artificial flowers became fashionable. Designers tried to outdo each other in their powers of invention, a rivalry that gave rise to fantasy jewellery. The technique of enamel-painting on gold ushered in a broader palette of colours, while decorative compositions were further enriched by the addition of pearls and gemstones.

Nitot's former workshop supervisor, Jean-Baptiste Fossin (1786–1848), became the official supplier to King Louis-Philippe,[10] representing the epitome of the virtuoso jeweller celebrated by the Parisian elite (even earning appearances in works by Honoré de Balzac, Alfred de Musset and Théophile Gautier). Although he sculpted busts and regularly exhibited paintings at the Salon, 'Fossin deserves special mention as a jeweller, because he was the first in his era to seek to embrace nature, via his lovely designs for the bouquets that he crafted in cut diamonds.'[11] Fossin did indeed draw inspiration from flowers he observed in fields and gardens, as well as from the ears of wheat that he drew from memory with a calligraphy pen, as is evident in his fuchsia brooch, bracelets adorned with foliage, and a gemstone bouquet mounted in silver (with gold stems) presented at the French industrial exhibition at the Louvre in 1819.

Fossin designed tiaras decorated with lush bouquets of ivy, vine and chestnut leaves, reeds, waterlilies and jasmine, combined with fruits including grapes, cherries and redcurrants. Plant motifs ranged from the ruby and cut-diamond geraniums created for Queen Marie-Amélie in 1847 to a hazelnut on a twig. Their realistic effect was enhanced by the inclusion of tiny springs that made the flowers of the tiara tremble with the movements of its wearer. There are countless other drawings of flowers, either in isolation or in bunches or garlands, that were intended for production in tinted ivory, painted enamel, porcelain, coral, cornelian or precious stones. The pair of so-called 'Mancini' [12] hair ornaments was inspired by the hairstyle of Louis XIV's famous mistress Marie Mancini, who was considered one of the most elegant women of her age. It represented a variation on a garland, with a couple of sprigs hanging down the cheeks, culminating in long fringes of diamond set off by other stones. Belt buckles were also decorated with natural motifs such as ivy, vine leaves and florets, or sharply rendered animal scenes showing, for example, dolphins in the midst of reeds, birds pecking at berries or dragons devouring snakes. A series of wild animal heads, echoing Antoine-Louis Barye's preparatory drawings for animal sculptures, were intended to be carved and mounted in pairs on golden bulrushes. In fact, wild animals were predominant – birds, reptiles, mammals and insects – embodying the Romantic ideal of unspoilt nature. The most popular animal in this period was by far the snake, a symbol of sentimental attachment and eternal love: its potential for endless variations fascinated Jean-Baptiste Fossin, just as it did the famous Romantic sculptors Auguste Clésinger and Barye.

The eclectic Second Empire

The marriage between Napoléon III and Eugénie de Montijo in 1853 marked the launch of a glittering court that glorified nature even more avidly through its taste in jewellery. Jules Fossin, who ran Chaumet until 1862 and served as jeweller to the imperial family, stood as 'one of the most artistic jewellers of the Second Empire period and produced works of a highly personal character'. [13] Following in the footsteps of his father, he made naturalistic tiaras that were veritable works of art, including his famous pansy tiara, created around 1850, which celebrated that most humble of flowers in a white monochrome arrangement of diamonds, gold and silver. There was an abiding fashion for jewellery adorned with flowers and leaves, worn in a décolletage or in the hair, and Fossin continued to design garlands inspired by nature, in keeping with Romantic tastes. The drawings from this period abound in Neoclassical jewels that evoked the reign of Louis XVI: miniature laurel wreaths and lotus flowers, as well as wild roses and daisies gathered in bunches, often held together by ribbons. The use of these 18th-century themes reflected the Empress's fondness for the era of Marie-Antoinette. The brooches and pendants with motifs of maidenhair ferns, Virginia creeper, lily of the valley and fuchsia are of a piece with the frilly dresses of the Second Empire, as well as with the numerous flower paintings of Eugène Delacroix, who was intrigued by all aspects of the natural world.

The plant kingdom even exerted an influence on the texture of jewels. Bracelets were made with gold engraved to look like bark and embellished with enamelled leaves and flowers made of precious stones and pearls. The star motif was also very popular, not only when offset by enamel

backgrounds of various colours but also when it appeared as a single ornament or in a group. It was equally well suited to tiaras, hairpins and brooches. Many women wore a diamond crescent (associated with the goddess Diana) in their hair, and Prosper Morel, Jules Fossin's successor, designed crescents in various shapes and sizes, as recorded in Chaumet's albums. Meanwhile, hunting themes were still in vogue, as represented by the heads of lions, wild boars, foxes and wolves, as well as hares, pheasants, partridges and ducks.

The aigrette made its first appearance during this period, and it offered a new opportunity for displaying natural themes. It was generally worn in the hair, although it could also be pinned to a black velvet toque at night. Large tortoiseshell combs adorned with flowers or leaves were sometimes set on top of women's hairstyles, which were worn very high. Earrings became much more common after 1860, and they also sported flowers and leaves (ivy, vines, fuchsia and jasmine) that hung quite naturally from the ears. Small brooches, in their turn, reproduced a wide range of humble flowers from fields and gardens – forget-me-nots, eglantines, pansies, violets, dahlias and orange blossoms – and leaves, including chestnut, geranium, parsley and fig. Similar flower and foliage motifs were also applied to jewelled pins.[14] A host of insects were also depicted, from flies and wasps to dragonflies and butterflies. This panoply of animal and plant motifs, found on all types of jewels, constitutes both a herbarium and a bestiary at Maison Chaumet and reveals how the house's reliance on the natural world as a source of inspiration reached its zenith in the 1860s.

The Belle Époque and Art Nouveau (1879–1914)

Although the plant and animal worlds continued to form major sources of inspiration for Art Nouveau in the late 19th and early 20th centuries, the iconography was refreshed, and themes including marine plantlife, seaweed, waterlilies, tropical creepers and climbing plants became new favourites. The roses that had been so popular in the first half of the 19th century were superseded by exotic flowers, orchids and chrysanthemums, although they were interpreted imaginatively rather than with scientific exactitude. René Lalique, considered the inventor of modern jewellery by his contemporaries, preferred field flowers to sophisticated plants, and chose metals and stones that fitted the composition he had in mind regardless of their market value: 'He was convinced that the art of setting was more important than the intrinsic value of the material being used.'[15] Jewellery design therefore broke away from its historical precedents and encouraged a free and personal interpretation of nature in which the design and composition determined the choice of materials. The designers at Chaumet learned from ornamentalists such as Eugène Grasset how to adapt forms and settings to objects destined for decoration. The *peineta* (high comb), inspired by Spanish tradition, is a perfect example of how a setting could be adapted: a chosen plant or flower determined both the form of the *peineta* and the decoration of its upper section (the part that was on display when worn in the hair).

This new aesthetic attracted the attention of Joseph Chaumet (1852–1928), who gave his name to the Maison and in 1907 set up shop at 12 Place Vendôme (thus establishing an epicentre for Parisian luxury brands). Chaumet came up with his own personal version, however, and he was extremely selective in his choice of motifs. Although he created nymphs, Medusa's heads and other seductive female figures, his preference was for simple flowers such as poppies, umbellifers and harebells, and elegant insects including dragonflies, grasshoppers, maybugs and decorative predators, as well as reptiles and bats. The iconography thus became more symbolic than naturalistic. Chaumet's preparatory study for the 'Cornflower, fruit blossom, pansy and butterfly' stomacher recalls watercolours by the painter Odilon Redon in its harmonious and naturalistic, but also dreamlike, combination of flowers and butterflies. Birds' wings became a fashionable subject right up to the early 1920s, inspired by the winged helmets worn by the Valkyries, the warrior divinities of Nordic mythology presented in the operas of Richard Wagner. They could be mounted on the top of the head, facing in all directions, on aigrettes or on brooches pinned on a bodice, either individually or in pairs. Customers who shared Joseph Chaumet's monarchist and Catholic convictions would often wear fleurs-de-lis (an emblem of the Bourbons) on aigrettes, combined with ostrich feathers. Chaumet adopted the aesthetic canons of Art Nouveau to present this highly distinctive iconography, creating stylised forms in delicate, freely rendered arabesques.

This magical, wondrous approach to drawing from nature, which sometimes gave birth to fantastic animals, was backed up by great technical mastery. Like René Lalique, Joseph Chaumet preferred platinum set with precious stones to enamelled gold. He also developed a system of moulds that made it possible to repeat and change a motif at will, along the lines of the moveable type used in printshops. This innovation allowed Chaumet to reproduce complex patterns on the surface of his jewels with greater ease, while also saving money. After throwing himself into the 1900 Universal Exposition, 'Chaumet felt that the beauty of an objet d'art did not reside in the multiplication of diverse elements, however pleasing and pretty they may be in isolation. The objective was rather an overall harmony, a general expressiveness, an eloquent simplicity – in short, a style.'[16] Joseph Chaumet acquired an international reputation for the elegance of his designs and the superior quality of his pearls[17] and precious stones, which he studied scientifically in his own laboratory. According to Diana Scarisbrick, 'Chaumet restored the primacy of gemstones. They ceased to be merely highlights and ornaments in small-scale allegorical, sentimental and rural compositions, in illustrations of picturesque scenes, in garlands, foliage, false wood or the produce of land or sea, and took on the starring role … the mount was effaced and lightened, becoming very sober and discreet. This principle is still guiding fashion today.'[18]

The Belle Époque also saw the Maison open up to visions from overseas. It was anxious to win the coveted custom of the Indian Maharajahs, so when, in late 1910, the Maharajah of Baroda requested an examination of his jewellery collection with the help of the technology developed by the Maison, Chaumet dispatched a team of experts, including the designer Henri Delaspre. Chaumet also contributed to an enormous commission from the Sultan of Morocco, Mawlay Abd al-Aziz, in 1902, comprising rings, bracelets, necklaces and other items. He also drew inspiration from Japanese art, with its unusual framings and delicate, modest and poetic emphasis on flowers, insects and birds. These outside influences served to enrich the repertoire of natural subjects that is so dear to the Maison.

'After the naturalism of Art Nouveau, nature was synthesised, before veering towards geometry.'[20] The period from the end of the First World War to the beginning of the 21st century was marked by profound social changes and lurches between financial booms and crashes; jewellery adapted to this new context and to prevailing fashions in clothes.

Art Deco: daring modernity

The decorative arts reflected all the aesthetic movements that sprung up around 1910, from geometrical abstraction to Cubism and Futurism – not to mention the theoretical debates of the inter-war years. Forms were simplified, and lines became bold, sharp and clean. Throughout this period, the designers at Chaumet kept a close eye on developments in haute couture. They took note of the boyish look adopted by women in the Roaring Twenties and created new jewellery to match. They interpreted the trend towards streamlined, geometric forms, incorporating strong colour contrasts and interplays between opacity and transparency. The emergence of platinum, which transformed the appearance of diamond jewellery, presaged a new era: historians have noted how 'platinum mounts were more malleable and discreet, leaving the focus on oppositions between coloured masses'.[21] In 1925 the International Exhibition of Modern Decorative and Industrial Arts in Paris had a worldwide impact and gave fresh inspiration to the designers who held court in the jewellery section in the Grand Palais. The brooches, belt buckles and other items displayed there by Maison Chaumet were remarkable for their severe geometrical lines and were set with stones of contrasting colours and varying sizes. Although these elements would take pride of place during the Art Deco period (at the expense of figurative representations of fauna and flora), there was still room for some of Chaumet's iconic motifs, such as bouquets and baskets of flowers and fruits, influenced by Oriental art. This plant-based iconography drew on recent botanical discoveries, which had opened up an inexhaustible repertoire of forms.[22]

Parisian designers had another opportunity to demonstrate their talent in 1929, in a major jewellery exhibition at the Palais Galliera.[23] The jewellery displayed there by Marcel Chaumet (1886–1964), who had succeeded his father the year before, was sculptural, geometrical and monochrome (completely white, in fact, owing to the application of layers of transparent and frosted rock crystal). These smoother colour combinations were in keeping with more feminine tailoring that emphasised the natural contours of the body, including the décolletage. This new style of clothing called for jewellery that was imposing in terms of both size and design, to add a touch of luxury that would otherwise be absent. Long necklaces that adorned both the décolletage and the back fulfilled this role perfectly, while an increase in the use of semi-precious stones – amethysts, aquamarines, garnets and topaz – was a sign of the ongoing financial crisis. (Gold did not entirely disappear, however, since it was less expensive than platinum.) Although tiaras in the form of a crown had become outdated and the traditional matching sets of tiara, earrings, necklace and bracelets were now reserved for royalty, jewellery for the hair – such as headbands, combs, clips and barrettes – still retained a degree of popularity.

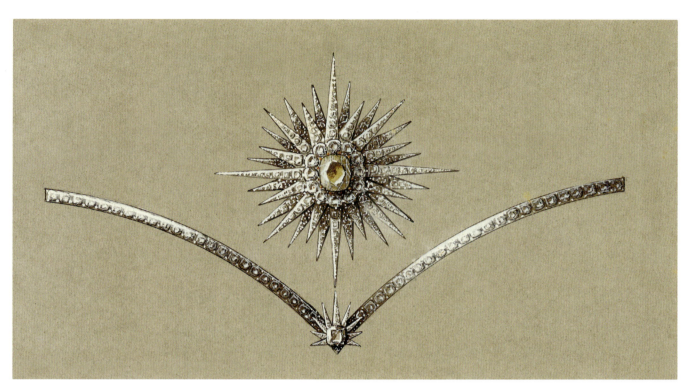

Two designs for sunburst aigrettes, Joseph Chaumet,
drawing studio, c. 1910, graphite pencil, gouache
and wash on translucent paper.

A new vision of nature: the 1940s

The Art Deco period was thus relatively insignificant as far as natural forms in jewellery are concerned, but in the late 1930s flower and plant motifs began to reappear, accompanied by a renewed taste for gold and for eye-catching colours. The Second World War, and the generally accepted understanding that gold would always maintain its value, led to the creation of bulkier jewellery, particularly extravagant rings. The jewellery of the 1940s was distinguished by an extreme stylisation of forms, along with voluptuous lines and swirling motifs.

The return of daisies, nasturtiums, anemones, roses and camellias was primarily due to the appearance of the clip,[24] which would go on to supplant the brooch a few years later. In fact, clips became as essential to a woman's wardrobe in the 1930s and 1940s as hats and shoes. Flower designs were sold singly or in bunches, made in platinum with diamonds or in gold with coloured stones. During the war, Chaumet enlarged its plant vocabulary to embrace cacti and reeds, while also adding parrots and birds of paradise to its avian repertoire. Its line of flowers and leaves that combined rose gold, white diamonds and coloured stones would endure until the late 1950s, in tone-on-tone or two-coloured bouquets.[25] This return to nature was, however, probably best exemplified by the tiara, which 'succeeded in remaining true to its original symbolic function as a ritual crown of flowers and leaves celebrating the cult of nature, swathing the foreheads of the victorious and honouring heads that stood out from the crowd'.[26]

Enduring themes from the 1950s onwards

Designs based on natural forms run through Chaumet's entire history, from the fashions of the Romantic period to its most recent collections. Ever since the 1950s, designers have struck a balance between the firm's traditions and the imperatives of modernisation, development and diversification. The thirty years of prosperity that followed the end of the Second World War enabled Chaumet to open branches overseas (as well as a new Parisian store with modern decor, *L'Arcade*), to create a heritage department and to promote itself via exhibitions, catalogues and advertising campaigns. Jewellery still adheres to traditional forms on account of the high value of its precious stones, but Chaumet has also introduced more accessible lines that are bolder in their design and use of materials. Its designers have the freedom to express themselves in a contemporary style, helping to democratise a Maison once renowned for its exclusiveness.[27]

From 1961 an unusual jeweller well ahead of his time, Pierre Sterlé (1905–1978), who was soon followed by René Morin (1932–2017), gave Chaumet a new creative sparkle and introduced fresh sources of inspiration. Both these artists produced designs based on nature that were daring, fantastical and free of constraints, as can be seen in the bulky forms and rough textures of their ginkgo and arum-lily necklaces. Many of Sterlé's projects demonstrate a playful if observant approach to the natural repertoire, as in the clips in the form of an arum lily, a starfish, a seahorse, a ram, a frog, a parrot or a hummingbird in flight.

Morin, in his turn, constantly drew on nature as a source of inspiration, thus establishing himself as the artistic heir to one of Chaumet's greatest jewellery directors, Jean-Valentin Morel. Morin was especially fond of fantastic creatures such as unicorns and the Minotaur, as well as further enriching Chaumet's range of seahorses, fish and horses. In 1968 Morin's research into raw materials led him to create a new technique: the production of *sauvage*, or 'raw gold'. This process involved working with gold to make it look as if it were in its natural state, either by giving it a matt finish or by polishing it vigorously. This technique was applied to torques embellished with various flowers and plants, thus bringing together Morin's twin passions of nature and raw materials. These necklaces were aimed at a new clientele that was not part of the haute bourgeoisie. In 1972 Morin joined forces with Baccarat, the crystal manufacturer, to produce the *Bestiaire fabuleux* series, which was based on residual pieces of raw glass left to cool after the furnace had been switched off. Morin used these random shapes to conjure up animal forms, both real and fantastic, that incorporated metals, pearls and stones, letting his imagination run wild.

By the start of the 1980s there was no longer much demand for tiaras or crowns: necklaces replaced them as the most important symbol of Chaumet's great heritage. Animal necklaces featuring swans, horses and panthers were produced from audacious designs using relatively inexpensive materials such as mother-of-pearl, coral and onyx. These unique creations tied in with the Maison's traditions by evoking the imperial jewels made by the Nitots (father and son) for Napoléon's two wives, which were the starting point for Chaumet's extraordinary story.

Even today, nature continues to inspire Chaumet's creations. Its designers preserve the legacy of the Nitots, Fossins and Morels by ensuring that the Maison dazzles as brightly as ever after two and a half centuries of existence. The 2016 *La Nature de Chaumet* collection put the spotlight back on the motifs of its glory days, particularly the oak tree, the lily, the laurel leaves used to crown conquerors, and the ears of wheat that symbolise prosperity. The *Les Ciels de Chaumet* collection (2019), in contrast, turned its gaze upwards to capture birds in flight, a sky glowing with sunshine and the moon surrounded by stars. These interpretations of nature created by the Maison are distinguished by their virtuosity, penchant for innovation and stylistic curiosity. Over and above any considerations of fashion, Chaumet remains proudly committed to its standards of excellence and, above all, to its signature style. What strikes the observer in Empress Joséphine's ears of wheat, the reed brooch produced by Joseph Chaumet around 1893 and the *Passion Incarnat* lily tiara from the 2016 *La Nature de Chaumet* collection is a remarkable sense of graphic and aesthetic continuity. And with its combination of straight lines and curves, the *Vertiges* tiara – conceived by Scott Armstrong in 2017 as 'nature transformed into architecture'[28] – stands as a symbol of this synthesis that nature drawings create.

Flowers

Above Design for a corsage brooch with wild roses, Joseph Chaumet,
drawing studio, c. 1890, gouache and wash on translucent paper.

Page 32 Design for a brooch in the form of a bouquet of hydrangeas with ribbon,
Joseph Chaumet, drawing studio, c. 1890, gouache and wash on translucent paper.

Flowers

'As symbols of the beauty of the world, flowers have taken on the sobering task of high-lighting the brevity of human existence. Their enchanting colours and bewitching scents are also metaphors for those sensual pleasures that Man is in danger of succumbing to every single day,' writes the art historian Joséphine Le Foll.[1] The ephemeral, soul-stirring beauty of flowers has been an everlasting source of inspiration not only for painters, but also for goldsmiths and jewellers. Empress Joséphine's boundless passion for flowers – which was translated onto paper by Pierre-Joseph Redouté (the flower painter at the Museum of Natural History, Paris) and transformed into jewellery by Marie-Étienne Nitot – meant that they became one of the favourite subjects of Chaumet's designers, whether in a state of continual, unbridled flux or constrained by horticulture. Flowers of all kinds were constantly studied – both whole, and in their component parts of pistils, stems and petals – before being reproduced and enhanced first on paper and then in metal and gemstones. Flowers transcended all class distinctions to stand as the symbol of female beauty, from imperial roses to delicate myosotis and wild bindweed, and from exuberant fuchsias to immaculate waterlilies. They provided jewellers with the perfect opportunity to pay homage to nature, either as decorative features or as protagonists, naturalistic or stylised, monochrome or multicoloured, on their own or gathered in a bouquet. Above all, flowers were perfect for making a visual impact, as a delicate support for dazzling pure colours that recalled the bouquets of Eugène Delacroix, the peonies of Édouard Manet, the anemones of Odilon Redon and the amaryllis of Piet Mondrian. While flow-ers embody the vitality of nature and the attributes of Flora, the goddess of spring, and of Ceres, the goddess of summer and abundance, they also have their own language, which was highlighted in pieces of sentimental jewellery. Unlike any other elements of the natural world, flowers stimulate the senses, inspire feelings, convey impressions and provoke reflection. Jules Fossin's pansies trigger memories and relieve heartache, while the carnations on Joseph Chaumet's tiaras evoke intense, pure love. Over and above their symbolism, flowers have achieved unexpected immortality through the art of jewellery design.

Design for a floral necklace, Joseph Chaumet, drawing studio, 1890–1900, ink, gouache, wash and gold pigment on translucent paper.

Flowers

Above Design for a corsage brooch with daisies,
Joseph Chaumet, drawing studio, c. 1890, graphite
pencil, gouache and wash on translucent paper.

Right Design for a narcissus corsage brooch,
Joseph Chaumet, drawing studio, c. 1890, gouache
and wash on translucent paper.

Opposite Design for a primula corsage brooch,
Joseph Chaumet, drawing studio, c. 1890, gouache
and wash on translucent paper.

Pansy

The pansy is related to the violet, even though they are two different species in the *Viola* genus. The pansy, which is the result of cross-breeding, is blessed with what is known as 'hybrid vigour'. Its large, brightly coloured flowers are often found in gardens. The pansy's thin, overlapping petals give the flower a distinctive concave shape that has made it a popular subject in the decorative arts. Its status as a symbol of memory and sentiment provided an added attraction for jewellers. Jean-Baptiste Fossin, for example, explored its forms in minute detail, creating an extraordinary pansy tiara for Chaumet in around 1850. The painter Henri Fantin-Latour also depicted the pansy in his works, while in 1857 the celebrated illustrator Grandville gave it a unique twist in his series called *Les Fleurs Animées*, in which every flower was endowed with a strikingly individual personality. · MARC JEANSON

Above Design for the transformable *Pensée* tiara in white and yellow gold, set with a yellow (Fancy Vivid Yellow VS2) 1.03 carat brilliant-cut diamond with yellow and brilliant-cut diamonds. *Le Jardin de Chaumet* collection, 2023.

Design for a pansy necklace, Joseph Chaumet, drawing studio,
c. 1900, graphite pencil, gouache and ink wash on translucent paper.

Design for a corsage brooch with poppy, Joseph Chaumet, drawing studio,
c. 1890, graphite, gouache and gold pigment on tinted paper.

Top Design for a corsage brooch with wild roses,
Joseph Chaumet, drawing studio, *c.* 1900, graphite pencil,
gouache and grey ink wash on tinted paper.

Above Design for an aigrette with hawthorn blossom,
Joseph Chaumet, drawing studio, *c.* 1900, graphite pencil, gouache
and grey ink wash on tinted paper.

Design for a michauxia brooch, Joseph Chaumet, drawing studio,
c. 1900, gouache and wash on waxed paper.

Flowering Rush

Chaumet's botanical repertoire is surprisingly wide-ranging, as can be seen from the substantial roll call of plant species recorded in the Maison's archives. Apart from the expected classics, a perusal of Chaumet's albums reveals clovers and thistles, as well as studies of seaweed: no plant is considered too humble to serve as a source of inspiration. The flowering rush is a relatively rare species in Europe (it is protected in various regions), having originally been introduced from South East Asia. It is an aquatic plant that can grow to a height of 1.5 metres (5 feet). The attractive white or pinkish flowers are arranged in umbels, while its leaves are sharply defined and linear. Chaumet's graphic artists were drawn particularly to the purity and elegance of its flowers. The flowering rush is found in watery areas alongside bulrushes and waterlilies, which also feature prominently in the Maison's archives. · MARC JEANSON

Above Design for a flowering rush (*Butomus umbellatus*) brooch, Joseph Chaumet, drawing studio, c. 1910, graphite pencil, gouache and wash on waxed paper.

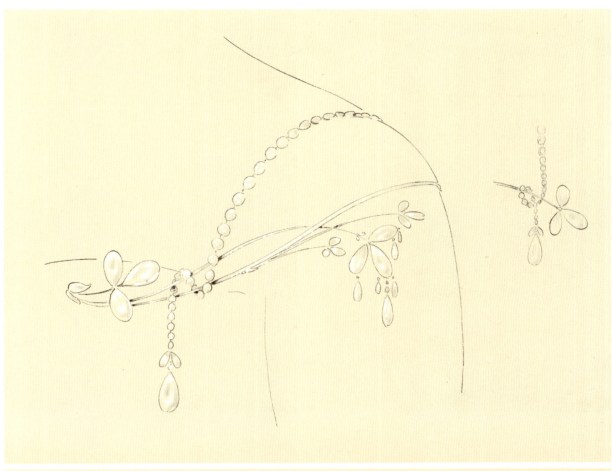

Opposite Design for a corsage brooch, Joseph Chaumet, drawing studio, *c.* 1900, graphite pencil, gouache and wash on tinted paper.

Top and above Two designs for clover shoulder ornaments, Joseph Chaumet, drawing studio, *c.* 1900, graphite pencil, gouache and wash on tinted paper.

Your hours are flowers intertwined with each other; do not pick off their petals before their time.

Victor Hugo, 'À une jeune fille', 1825

Above Design for floral tiara, Joseph Chaumet, drawing studio,
c. 1890, graphite pencil and gouache on tinted paper.

Top Design for a daisy aigrette, Joseph Chaumet, drawing studio, 1898, graphite pencil and gouache on tinted paper.

Above Design for a wild rose aigrette, Joseph Chaumet, drawing studio, c. 1900, graphite pencil and gouache on tinted paper.

Top Design for a peony brooch, Joseph Chaumet,
drawing studio, *c.* 1890, graphite pencil, pen and grey ink,
gouache and ink wash on tinted paper.

Above Design for a corsage brooch with bindweed,
Joseph Chaumet, drawing studio, *c.* 1890, graphite pencil, pen
and grey ink, gouache and ink wash on tinted paper.

Waterlily

One of the best-known aquatic plants, the waterlily has great symbolic meaning. Its roots, which are anchored in the silt of slow-moving bodies of water, give rise to pure, colourful flowers that blossom on the water's surface. The blooms last for only a few hours, however, before they disappear under the surface. In the second half of the 19th century, the hybridisation of the rustic European white waterlily with dazzling tropical species extended the colour range of waterlilies that could survive in temperate climates. The results of these experiments, undertaken by both botanists and nursery owners, were presented at the Paris Universal Exhibition in 1889, where they so captivated Claude Monet that he decided to grow waterlilies in his own garden in Giverny. His many paintings of waterlilies are testament to his ongoing fascination with these flowers. The yellow waterlily, which is common in Europe, was also a key motif in the work of Art Nouveau craftsmen from Nancy, particularly in the furniture of Louis Majorelle. · MARC JEANSON

Above Design for a waterlily brooch, Joseph Chaumet, drawing studio, c. 1900, pen and black ink, gouache and wash on tinted paper.

fleurs naturelles

1415

Above Peony flower, Joseph Chaumet, photography lab, before 1904, silver gelatin print from glass plate negative.

Opposite Design for a floral necklace with poppies and daisies, Joseph Chaumet, drawing studio, c. 1890, graphite pencil, watercolour, pen and grey ink on tinted paper.

Overleaf, left Design for a necklace with poppies and wildflowers, Joseph Chaumet, drawing studio, c. 1890, gouache and wash on tinted paper.

Overleaf, right Design for a necklace with wheat-ears and poppies, Joseph Chaumet, drawing studio, c. 1890, gouache and wash on tinted paper.

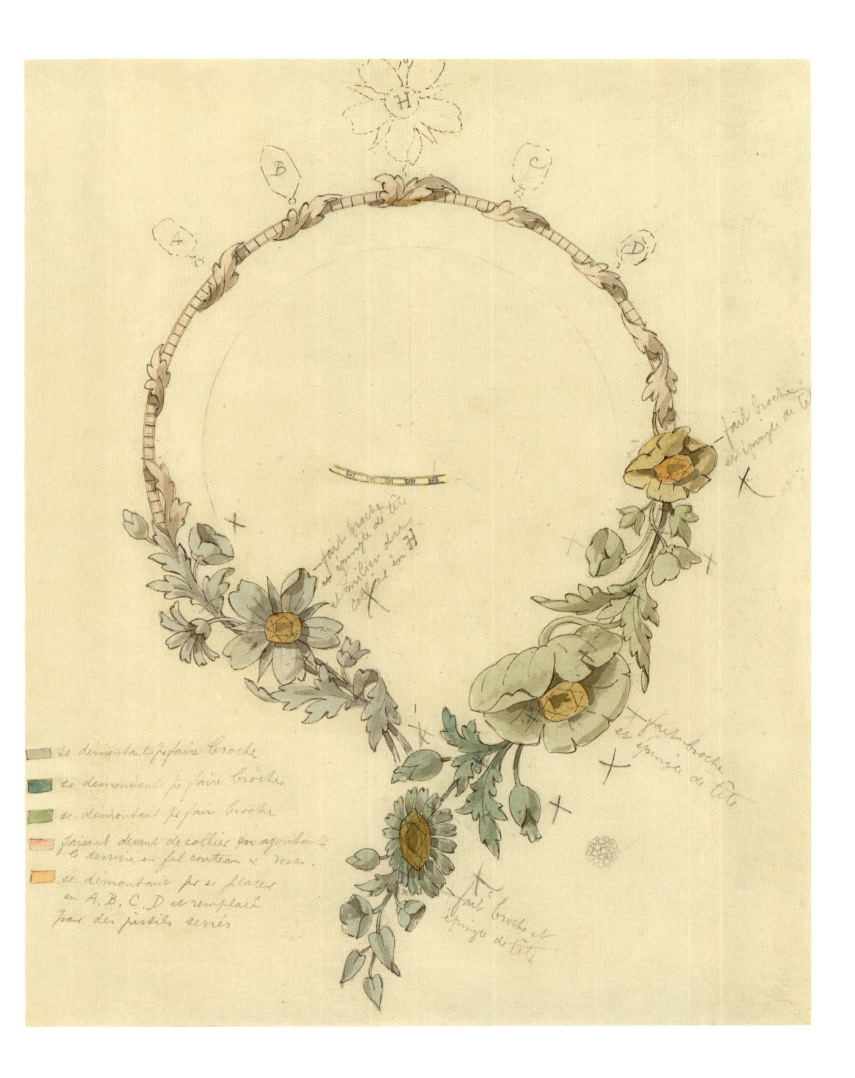

Top Design for a corsage brooch with chrysanthemums, Joseph Chaumet, drawing studio, c. 1890–1900, graphite pencil, gouache and wash on tinted paper.

Above Design for a corsage brooch with roses, Joseph Chaumet, drawing studio, c. 1890–1900, graphite pencil, pen, gouache and wash on tinted paper.

Design for a corsage brooch with wild roses, Joseph Chaumet, drawing studio,
c. 1890, graphite pencil, gouache, wash and gum arabic on tinted paper.

Design for the transformable *Iris* necklace in white gold, set with a 24.26 carat cushion-cut rose spinel, fancy-cut padparadscha sapphires, fancy-cut rose spinels, and baguette-cut and brillant-cut diamonds. *Le Jardin de Chaumet* collection, 2023.

Every flower is a soul blooming in nature.

Gérard de Nerval, 'Vers dorés' from *Odelettes*, 1853

Above Iris flowers, Joseph Chaumet, photography lab, c. 1900,
silver gelatin print from a glass plate negative.

Two designs for daisy tiaras, Joseph Chaumet, drawing studio, c. 1900,
graphite pencil and gouache on translucent paper.

Design for a double-row necklace with floating gemstones and floral motifs, Joseph Chaumet, drawing studio, c. 1890, graphite pencil and gouache on translucent paper.

Top Design for a corsage brooch with
jasmine flower, Joseph Chaumet, drawing studio,
c. 1900, gouache and wash on tinted paper.

Above Design for a cloverleaf aigrette-tiara
Joseph Chaumet, drawing studio, *c.* 1900,
graphite pencil, pen and brown ink, gouache
and ink wash on tinted paper.

Right Tulip study for a large brooch,
Joseph Chaumet, drawing studio, *c.* 1890,
gouache and wash on tinted paper.

Opposite Design for the transformable *Tulipe*
necklace in white gold, set with a 10.80 carat pear-cut
red spinel, a 1.01 carat pear-cut E VVS2 diamond,
calibrated red spinels, round-cut mandarin garnets,
and calibrated and brilliant-cut diamonds.
Le Jardin de Chaumet collection, 2023.

Design for an orchid necklace, Joseph Chaumet, drawing studio,
c. 1890, gouache and wash on translucent paper.

Design for an orchid necklace, Joseph Chaumet, drawing studio,
c. 1890, gouache and wash on translucent paper.

Orchid

This iconic plant displays an extraordinarily diverse range of colours and forms. It can be found in many parts of the world but it particularly thrives in the tropics, especially rainforests. These habitats are home to not only terrestrial orchids, but also epiphytic species that produce aerial roots and grow on the branches of host trees. New varieties of orchids emerged in the 19th century: advances in horticultural techniques allowed them to be bred in Europe, where numerous hybrids were created. The orchid is a symbol of love, elegance, ardour and sexuality. It has fascinated collectors, as well as scientists such as Charles Darwin, artists such as Émile Gallé (who studied orchids in great detail) and writers including Marcel Proust, who used orchids as a metaphor in his novel *In Search of Lost Time*. · MARC JEANSON

Above left Design for a lily brooch, Joseph Chaumet, drawing studio, c. 1890, gouache and wash on translucent paper.

Above right Design for an orchid brooch, Joseph Chaumet, drawing studio, c. 1890, gouache and wash on translucent paper.

Opposite Orchid aigrette, Joseph Chaumet, photography lab, before 1904, silver gelatin print from glass plate negative.

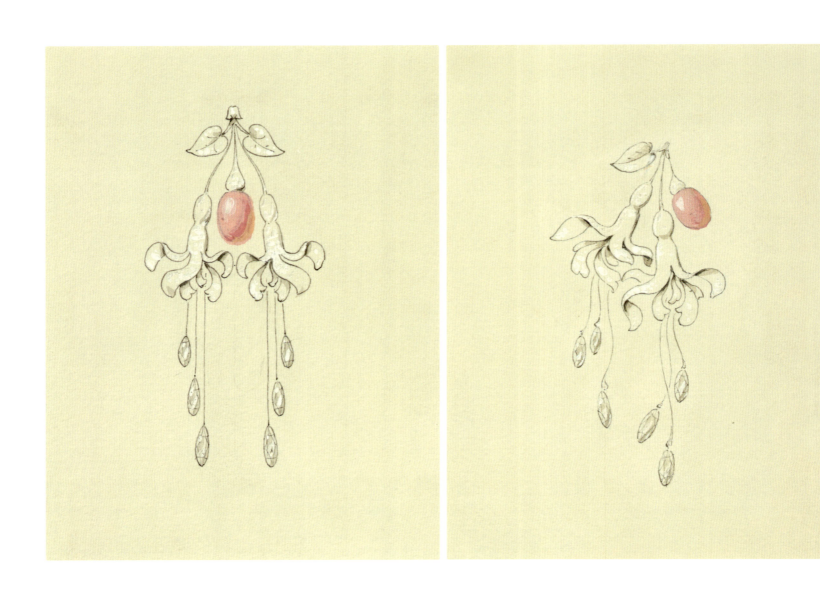

Two designs for a fuchsia brooch, Joseph Chaumet,
drawing studio, c. 1900–10, graphite pencil, pen and grey ink,
with ink and gouache wash on tinted paper.

Top Design for a floral tiara with conch pearls,
Joseph Chaumet, drawing studio, *c.* 1900–10, gouache,
graphite pencil, pen and grey ink, with ink and
gouache wash on tinted paper.

Above Design for a tiara with scabious flowers,
Joseph Chaumet, drawing studio, *c.* 1900–10, gouache,
graphite pencil, pen and grey ink, with ink and
gouache wash on tinted paper.

Opposite Design for a floral necklace with bindweed and cornflowers, Joseph Chaumet, drawing studio, *c.* 1890, graphite pencil, pen and brown ink, with ink and gouache wash on tinted paper.

Above Design for a lily of the valley brooch, Joseph Chaumet, drawing studio, *c.* 1900, graphite pencil, gouache and wash on tinted paper.

Left Design for a wild rose brooch, Joseph Chaumet, drawing studio, *c.* 1890, graphite pencil, pen and grey ink, with ink and gouache wash on tinted paper.

Designs for corsage brooches,
Joseph Chaumet, drawing studio,
c. 1890–1900, graphite pencil, gouache
and ink wash on translucent paper.

73

Design for a chrysanthemum tiara, Joseph Chaumet, drawing studio, c. 1880–1910,
graphite pencil, pen and grey ink, with ink and gouache wash on tinted paper.

Trees and Plants

Above Design for a corsage brooch with laurel leaves, Joseph Chaumet,
drawing studio, c. 1890, graphite pencil, gouache and wash on tinted paper.

Page 76 Leaf studies of clematis, buttercup, wild strawberry,
hawthorn, ivy and bindweed, Joseph Chaumet, drawing studio, c. 1885,
graphite pencil, gouache and wash on translucent paper.

Trees
and Plants

Although plant life, be it wild or domesticated, has inspired artists since ancient times, it really came into its own in jewellery design in the 17th century, following the emergence of the still life as a pictorial genre and, later on, a popular craze for botany and the natural sciences. The audacity of Maison Chaumet is evident in both its unfailing preference for iconic, deeply symbolic plants, such as wheat, vines and oaks, and its insatiable curiosity concerning modest, sometimes little-known plants including ivy, holly, clover, thistles, oats, reeds and ferns. Drawing inspiration not only from gardens but also from the undergrowth (even the tiniest weeds), Chaumet has taken an original view of the plant world and focused on species that have hitherto been spurned. Its designers are attracted by the plants' aesthetic qualities, just as the Romantic painter Eugène Delacroix drew foliage and bindweed, and the Impressionist Édouard Manet felt free to paint cucumbers and jars of asparagus. In the world of art and design, untamed aspects of nature are ideally suited to experimentation, especially their form and colour – although few plant motifs have marked the history of the decorative arts as much as the acanthus scroll, found on Corinthian columns from the 5th century BCE right up to the Napoleonic period. This thorny plant, which represents triumph over adversity, became a staple motif in jewellery design and was popular with Chaumet until the Belle Époque. Back in the 18th century the ear of wheat, which is also a symbol of fertility, prosperity and constant renewal (in France, it is historically associated with the nurturing role of the Republic), featured on the seal of the Maison's founder, Marie-Étienne Nitot. It was also the favourite motif of Empress Joséphine, who wore it on a tiara. In the Romantic period, the ear of wheat became a popular motif worn on the crown of the head, as part of a garland on the forehead, or as a brooch. In the 1850s Jules Fossin was particularly drawn to the vine, as much for its associated symbolism of abundance and vitality as for the decorative outline of its leaves. Chaumet's jewellers also turned their attention to more modest (and thus less commonly reproduced) elements, such as oak, ivy and clover leaves, and sprigs of reeds, oats and redcurrants. These emblems appeared most frequently on tiaras and headdresses. Moving forward to 2017, Scott Armstrong – who studied at Central Saint Martins in London and is today a designer at the Maison – won a competition organised by Chaumet to design a new tiara. He chose the theme of the 'French garden', combining the elegant classicism of straight flowerbeds with an abstract treatment of flower shapes to produce a piece entitled *Vertiges*. This deliberate contrast summarised almost 200 years of botanical inspiration and gave fresh impetus to Chaumet's long-standing tradition of observing plant species, from the most illustrious to the humblest.

Trees and Plants

Opposite Design for an ivy corsage brooch, Joseph Chaumet, drawing studio, c. 1900, graphite pencil, pen and brown ink, with gouache and ink wash on tinted paper.

Myriad rubies
and myriad pearls,
Clasp the waves of
her two blonde braids,
My heart rejoices
at her happiness.

Pierre de Ronsard, 'Les amours', 1553

Overleaf, above
Design for a tiara with oats motif,
Joseph Chaumet, drawing studio,
c. 1900–10, graphite pencil, pen and
grey ink, with gouache and ink
wash on tinted paper.

Overleaf, below
Design for a tiara with grasses motif,
Joseph Chaumet, drawing studio,
c. 1900–10, graphite pencil, pen
and grey ink, with gouache and
ink wash on tinted paper.

Opposite Design for a carnation tiara,
Joseph Chaumet, drawing studio, 1900–10,
graphite pencil, pen and brown ink, with
gouache and ink wash on tinted paper.

Above Design for a ginkgo-leaf
brooch, Joseph Chaumet, drawing
studio, c. 1900–10, graphite pencil,
pen and grey ink, with gouache
and ink wash on tinted paper.

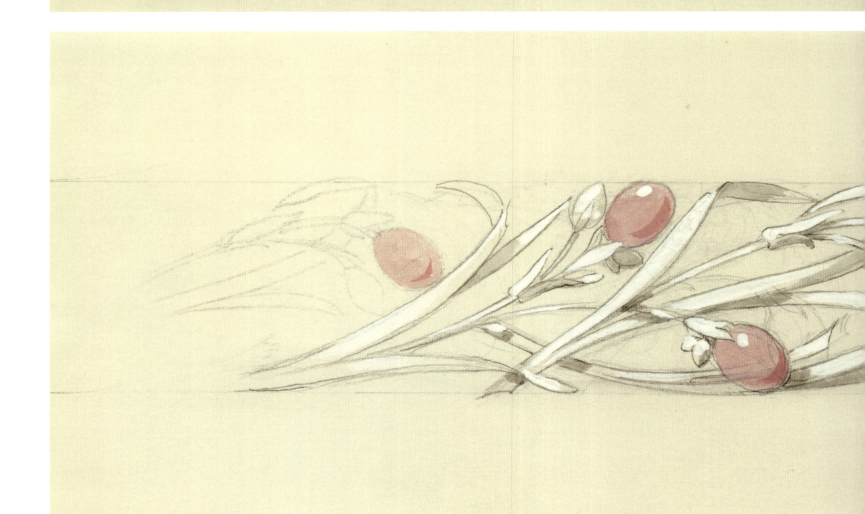

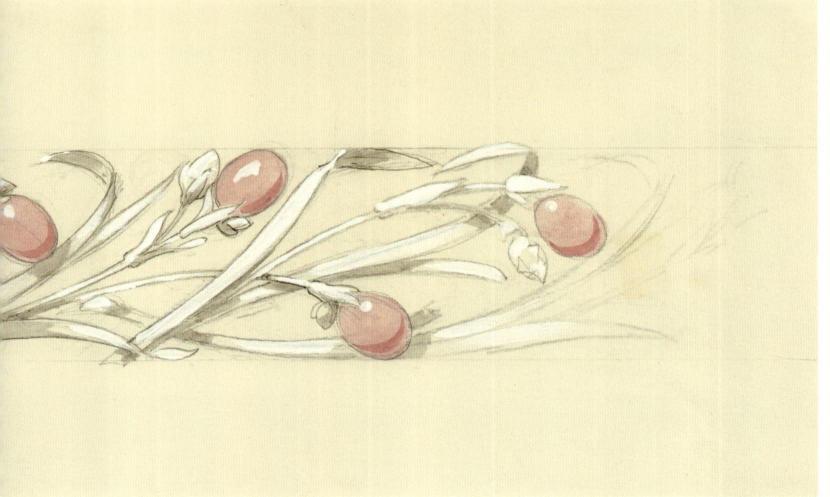

Two designs for a corsage
brooch with holly leaves, Joseph Chaumet,
drawing studio, c. 1900, gouache and
wash on tinted paper.

Top Design for a floral brooch,
Joseph Chaumet, drawing studio, *c.* 1890,
gouache and wash on tinted paper.

Above Three designs for fern brooches,
Joseph Chaumet, drawing studio, 1890–1900,
gouache and wash on tinted paper.

Vines

The grapevine is a creeper whose ancient wild ancestor was domesticated around 8,000 years ago somewhere between the Black Sea and Iran. It is a very vigorous plant that deploys powerful tendrils to attach itself to a vertical support. Some genera, such as the so-called 'Boston ivy', have small adhesive pads that enable their stems to stick to a support. Vine leaves can vary enormously in shape even on a single plant, let alone the thousands of different varieties in existence. The vine's slender, graceful form, attractive leaves, flexible tendrils and heavy bunches of fruit, along with its symbolic connection to wine, have all made it a common motif in a wide range of artistic media. The Baroque painter Bartolomeo Bimbi captured the diversity of grapes and vine leaves in his lavish still lifes, most of which were painted to decorate the villas of the Medici. The vine recurs frequently in the work of Maison Chaumet, which has observed the plant in great detail and skilfully rendered its forms and details by means of gemstones, metals and techniques such as painted enamel. · MARC JEANSON

Above Design for a corsage brooch with grapes and vine leaves, Joseph Chaumet, drawing studio, c. 1890, graphite pencil and gouache on tinted paper.

Opposite Design for the *Feuille de Vigne* necklace in white gold, set with a 5.18 carat cushion-cut Mozambique ruby, black and grey calibrated spinels, and fancy- and brilliant-cut diamonds. *Le Jardin de Chaumet* collection, 2023.

Above Design for a corsage brooch with grapes,
Joseph Chaumet, drawing studio, 1890–1900,
gouache and wash on tinted paper.

Opposite Corsage brooch with grapes and vine leaves,
Joseph Chaumet, photography lab, c. 1890–1900, silver
gelatin print from glass plate negative.

Above Design for a wild rose corsage brooch,
Joseph Chaumet, drawing studio, *c.* 1900, graphite
pencil with gouache and ink wash on tinted paper.

Right Design for an ivy corsage brooch,
Joseph Chaumet, drawing studio, *c.* 1910, graphite
pencil with gouache wash on tinted paper.

Top Design for an oak-branch corsage brooch,
Joseph Chaumet, drawing studio, c. 1890,
gouache and wash on tinted paper.

Above Design for a floral tiara, Joseph Chaumet,
drawing studio, c. 1900, graphite pencil,
gouache and wash on tinted paper.

Top Design for an ivy tiara,
Joseph Chaumet, drawing studio,
c. 1910, graphite pencil, gouache
and wash on tinted paper.

Above Design for a fern and ivy
diamond tiara, Joseph Chaumet,
c. 1910, graphite pencil, gouache
and wash on tinted paper.

Opposite Design for an ivy corsage
brooch, Joseph Chaumet, drawing
studio, *c.* 1910, graphite pencil,
gouache and wash on tinted paper.

Opposite, above Diamond fern and ivy tiara,
Joseph Chaumet, photography lab, 1910, silver
gelatin print from glass plate negative.

Above Two designs for ivy tiaras, Joseph Chaumet,
drawing studio, *c.* 1890, graphite pencil, gouache
and wash on tinted paper.

Opposite, below Design for an ivy and fern tiara,
Joseph Chaumet, drawing studio, *c.* 1910, graphite
pencil, gouache and wash on tinted paper.

Above Two designs for tiaras with redcurrant berries,
Joseph Chaumet, drawing studio, c. 1890, graphite
pencil, gouache and ink on tinted paper.

Opposite, above Design for a palm-leaf tiara,
Joseph Chaumet, drawing studio, c. 1900, graphite
pencil and gouache on tinted paper.

Opposite, below Design for an orchid tiara,
Joseph Chaumet, drawing studio, c. 1890, graphite
pencil, gouache and ink on tinted paper.

Maquettes 1209 - 1209 bis

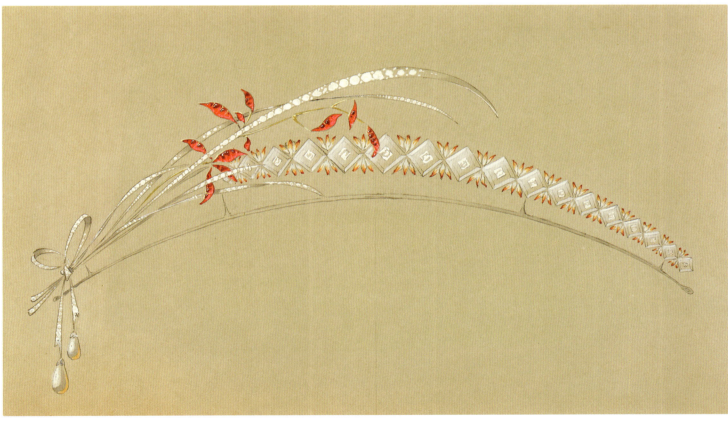

Above and opposite Three designs for bulrush aigrettes,
Joseph Chaumet, drawing studio, *c.* 1900, graphite pencil, pen and
brown ink, with gouache and ink wash on tinted paper.

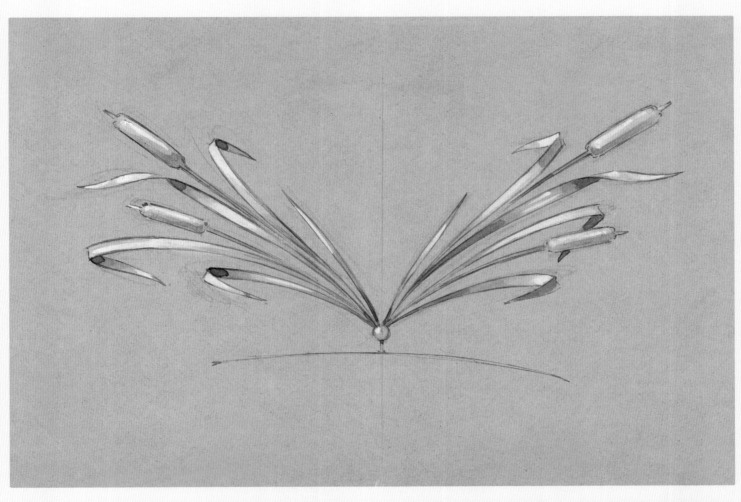

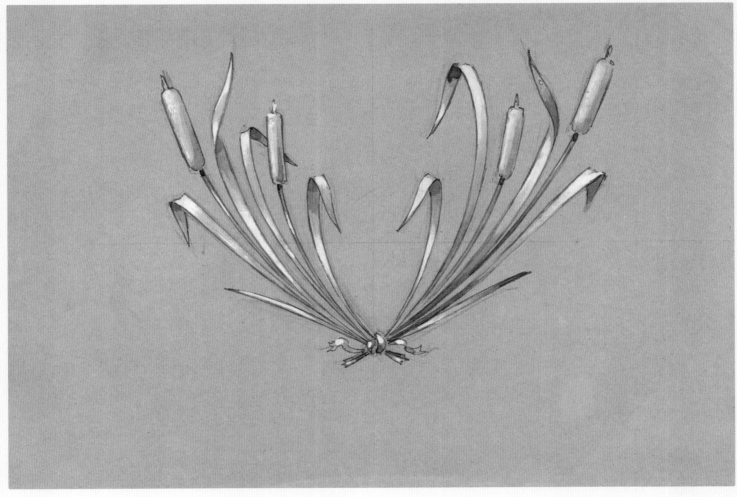

Let the moaning
wind, let the
sighing reed,
Let the delicate
scent of your
fragrant air,
Let everything
we hear, see
and breathe,
Let them
all say:
They loved!

Alphonse de Lamartine, 'Le lac', 1820

Left Design for a bulrush corsage brooch,
Joseph Chaumet, drawing studio, c. 1880, graphite
pencil, gouache and wash on translucent paper.

Opposite Design for a chrysanthemum corsage
brooch, Joseph Chaumet, drawing studio, c. 1890,
graphite pencil and gouache on tinted paper.

Opposite, left Design for a corsage brooch with
dragonfly and bulrushes, Joseph Chaumet, drawing
studio, c. 1880, graphite pencil, pen and grey ink, gouache
and ink wash with gum arabic on tinted paper.

Opposite, right Design for a corsage brooch with
bulrushes, Joseph Chaumet, drawing studio, c. 1880,
graphite pencil, pen and black ink, gouache and
ink wash, with gum arabic on tinted paper.

Left Design for a floral corsage brooch with
butterfly, Joseph Chaumet, drawing studio, c. 1890–1900,
graphite pencil, gouache and wash with gum
arabic on tinted paper.

Above Design for a corsage brooch with laurel leaves
and butterfly, Joseph Chaumet, drawing studio,
c. 1890, pen and black ink, gouache and ink wash
with gum arabic on grey tinted paper.

Two designs for ivy tiaras, Joseph Chaumet, drawing studio,
c. 1910, graphite pencil, gouache and wash on tinted paper.

Two designs for bulrush tiaras, Joseph Chaumet, drawing studio,
c. 1910, graphite pencil, gouache and wash on tinted paper.

Top Design for a ginkgo-leaf tiara, Joseph Chaumet, drawing studio, *c.* 1900, graphite pencil, gouache and ink on tinted paper.

Above Design for a floral tiara, Joseph Chaumet, drawing studio, *c.* 1900, graphite pencil, gouache and ink on tinted paper.

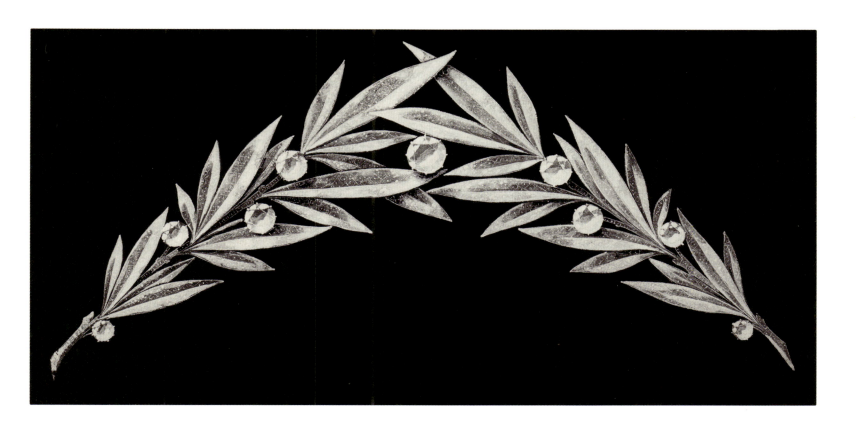

Two designs for laurel tiaras, Joseph Chaumet,
drawing studio, c. 1890–1905, graphite pencil,
black ink and gouache on tinted paper.

Still beneath Virgil's laurel bough,
The pale hortensia entwines
with the green myrtle!

Gérard de Nerval, 'Myrtho', 1854

Design for a laurel tiara, Joseph Chaumet, drawing studio, 1890,
graphite pencil, pen and brown ink, gouache and ink wash on tinted paper.

Design for a wheat-ear tiara, Joseph Chaumet, drawing studio,
c. 1900–10, graphite pencil and gouache on tinted paper.

Wheat-ear tiara, François-Regnault Nitot,
c. 1811, gold, silver and diamonds.

The morning sun casts a soft and golden light
On the rye and wheat still wet with dew,
And the blue sky retains the cool of the night.

Paul Verlaine, 'La bonne chanson', 1870

Above Design for a wheat-ear aigrette tiara,
Joseph Chaumet, drawing studio, c. 1890–1900,
graphite pencil, pen and brown ink, gouache
and ink wash on translucent paper.

Opposite Gouache design for the *Offrandes d'été*
bandeau in white gold, set with a 3.01 carat pear-cut
D VVS2 diamond and brilliant-cut diamonds.
La Nature de Chaumet collection, 2016.

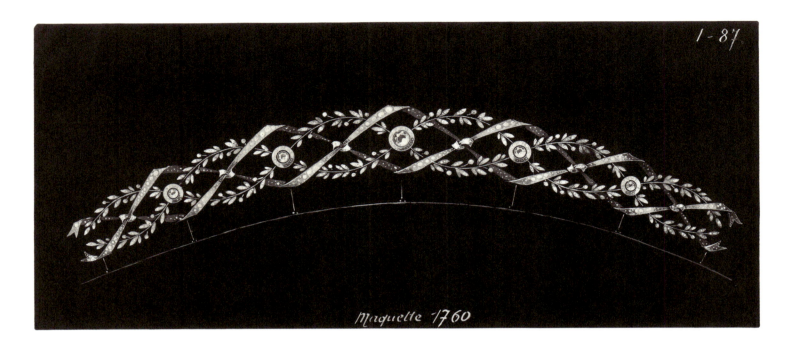

Maquette 1760

Top Design for a laurel choker transformable
into a bandeau, Joseph Chaumet, drawing studio, c. 1905,
graphite pencil, gouache and wash on tinted paper.

Above Design for laurel tiara, Joseph Chaumet,
drawing studio, c. 1900, graphite pencil and
gouache on tinted paper.

Opposite, above Design for a laurel tiara,
Joseph Chaumet, drawing studio, c. 1900, graphite
pencil and gouache on tinted paper.

Opposite, below Design for a bandeau tiara with leaf
motifs, Joseph Chaumet, drawing studio, c. 1900–10,
graphite pencil, gouache and wash on tinted paper.

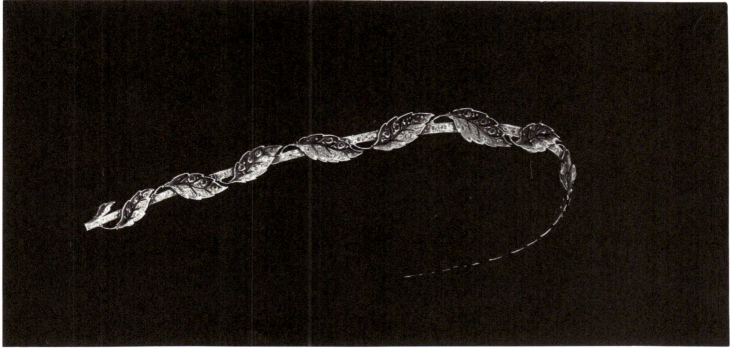

Design for the *Gui* necklace in white gold, set with a 21.59 carat cushion-cut Colombian emerald, natural pearls, and calibrated and brilliant-cut diamonds. *Le Jardin de Chaumet* collection, 2023.

Mistletoe

Mistletoe is a semi-parasitic plant that grows on the upper branches of trees such as oaks and poplars. Birds drop the berries from their beaks; on germination, the seedling penetrates the bark of the host tree to gain access to the sap. Once this connection has been established, the plant starts to grow thick, deep-green stems with broad leaves, which later sprout spherical, opaque white fruits. The pearly berries of mistletoe, as well as its geometric branching stem and thick leaves, have inspired a wide range of artists. These include painters such as André Derain, whose watercolours of mistletoe were the result of patient observation, as well as jewellers such as Joseph Chaumet and the craftsmen of the Nancy School, who incorporated it into designs for a wide range of ceramics, chandeliers and other objects. This fascinating plant was also highly valued by generations of Druids in Europe for its supposed magical and therapeutic properties. · MARC JEANSON

Above Design for a mistletoe tiara, Joseph Chaumet, drawing studio,
c. 1910, graphite pencil, gouache and wash on tinted paper.

Three designs for mistletoe brooches, Joseph Chaumet, drawing studio,
c. 1890–1900, gouache and wash on tinted paper.

Two designs for a mistletoe corsage brooch, Joseph Chaumet, drawing studio, c. 1900,
graphite pencil, pen and grey ink with ink wash and gouache on tinted paper.

If only I were
a leaf curled
by the twisting
wing of the wind,
That floats
upon the
flowing stream,
And is followed
by dreaming
eyes

Victor Hugo, 'Vœu', 1829

Opposite, above Design for a mistletoe brooch,
Joseph Chaumet, drawing studio, c. 1900, graphite
pencil. gouache and wash on translucent paper.

Opposite, below Design for a clover brooch,
Joseph Chaumet, drawing studio, c. 1900, gouache
and wash on translucent paper.

Right, top and centre Designs for ginkgo brooches,
Joseph Chaumet, drawing studio, c. 1900, gouache
and wash on translucent paper.

Right, below Design for a clover brooch,
Joseph Chaumet, drawing studio, c. 1900, gouache
and wash on translucent paper.

Above and opposite Two designs for clover combs,
Joseph Chaumet, drawing studio, c. 1890–1900, graphite
pencil and gouache on translucent paper.

Above Design for a comb with diamonds and teardrop emeralds, with leaf motifs, Joseph Chaumet, drawing studio, *c.* 1890–1900, graphite pencil and gouache on translucent paper.

Opposite, above Design for a comb with leaf motifs, Joseph Chaumet, drawing studio, *c.* 1890–1900, graphite pencil and gouache on translucent paper.

Opposite, below Design for a comb with alternating rows of leaf motifs and sapphires, Joseph Chaumet, drawing studio, *c.* 1890–1900, graphite pencil and gouache on tinted paper.

Above Two bracelet designs with a central emerald
and leaf motifs, Joseph Chaumet, drawing studio, *c.* 1900,
graphite pencil, gouache and ink on tinted paper.

Opposite Three designs for clover bracelets,
Joseph Chaumet, drawing studio, *c.* 1890, graphite
pencil and gouache on translucent paper.

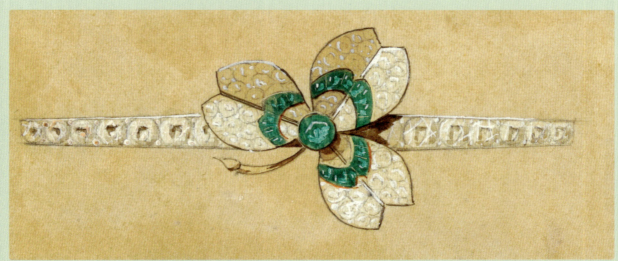

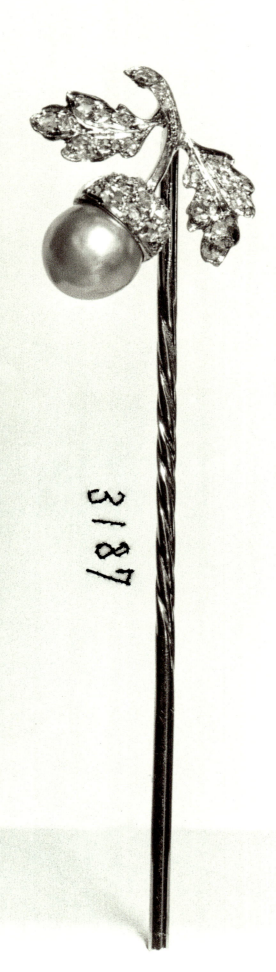

Oak

The oak is one of the largest and most common of European trees, particularly in the woodlands of France. There are, however, many subspecies that grow in both arid and humid subtropical regions, and even in tropical forests at high altitudes. For thousands of years, the oak has been associated symbolically with power, longevity and justice. The history of both the decorative and fine arts is studded with depictions of the oak's acorns, buds, leaves and canopy, including one of Gustave Courbet's most outstanding works, *The Oak at Flagey*, as well as glass vases designed by Émile Gallé. The oak has also been used extensively in architectural ornamentation. The Chaumet archives feature it in jewellery designs for both women (tiaras and necklaces) and men (tie pins). · MARC JEANSON

Opposite Hairpin with oak leaves and acorn, Joseph Chaumet, photography lab, c. 1890–1900, silver gelatin print from glass plate negative.

Above Design for a brooch with oak leaves and acorn, Joseph Chaumet, drawing studio, c. 1890, ink with gouache and ink wash on tinted paper.

Top Design for an oak-leaf tiara,
Joseph Chaumet, drawing studio,
c. 1910, graphite pencil, gouache
and wash on tinted paper.

Above Oak-leaf and acorn tiara,
Joseph Chaumet, photography lab,
c. 1890–1900, silver gelatin print
from glass plate negative.

Opposite Design for an oak-leaf corsage
brooch, Joseph Chaumet, drawing studio,
c. 1890, pen and black ink, gouache
and wash on tinted paper.

Design for an oak-leaf tiara, Joseph Chaumet, drawing studio, c. 1900,
graphite pencil, pen and brown ink, with gouache and ink wash on tinted paper.

Streaming
from leaf to leaf,
A reverberating
ray of light,
Among the lily
petals I strip off,
Slipping,
sliding and
pooling into
a lake of
brightness.

Alphonse de Lamartine
'Cantique sur un rayon de soleil', 1839

Opposite Designs for laurel corsage brooches,
Joseph Chaumet, drawing studio, c. 1900, graphite
pencil, gouache and wash on tinted paper.

Right Design for a laurel corsage brooch,
Joseph Chaumet, drawing studio, c. 1900, graphite
pencil, pen and black ink with gouache and
ink wash on tinted paper.

Top Design for a laurel-branch tiara, Joseph Chaumet, drawing studio, 1900–10, graphite pencil and gouache on tinted paper.

Above Design for an oak-leaf tiara, Joseph Chaumet, drawing studio, c. 1890–1900, graphite pencil and gouache on tinted paper.

Opposite, above Design for a laurel-branch tiara, Joseph Chaumet, drawing studio, 1890–1900, graphite pencil and gouache on tinted paper.

Opposite, below Design for a tiara with bulrushes and grasses, Joseph Chaumet, drawing studio, c. 1890–1900, graphite pencil and gouache on tinted paper.

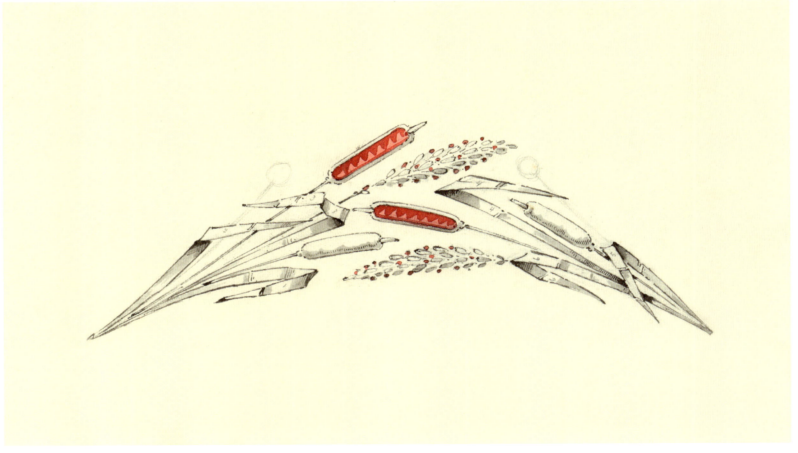

Design for a laurel necklace, Joseph Chaumet,
drawing studio, c. 1900, gouache and
wash on translucent paper.

Design for a clover necklace, Joseph Chaumet,
drawing studio, c. 1900, gouache and
wash on translucent paper.

Top Design for a four-leaf-clover brooch, Joseph Chaumet, drawing studio, *c.* 1890, gouache and wash on translucent paper.

Above Design for a cinquefoil brooch, Joseph Chaumet, drawing studio, *c.* 1890, graphite pencil, gouache and ink wash on translucent paper.

Right Design for a corsage brooch with bulrushes and dragonfly, Joseph Chaumet, drawing studio, *c.* 1880, graphite pencil, gouache and ink wash on tinted paper.

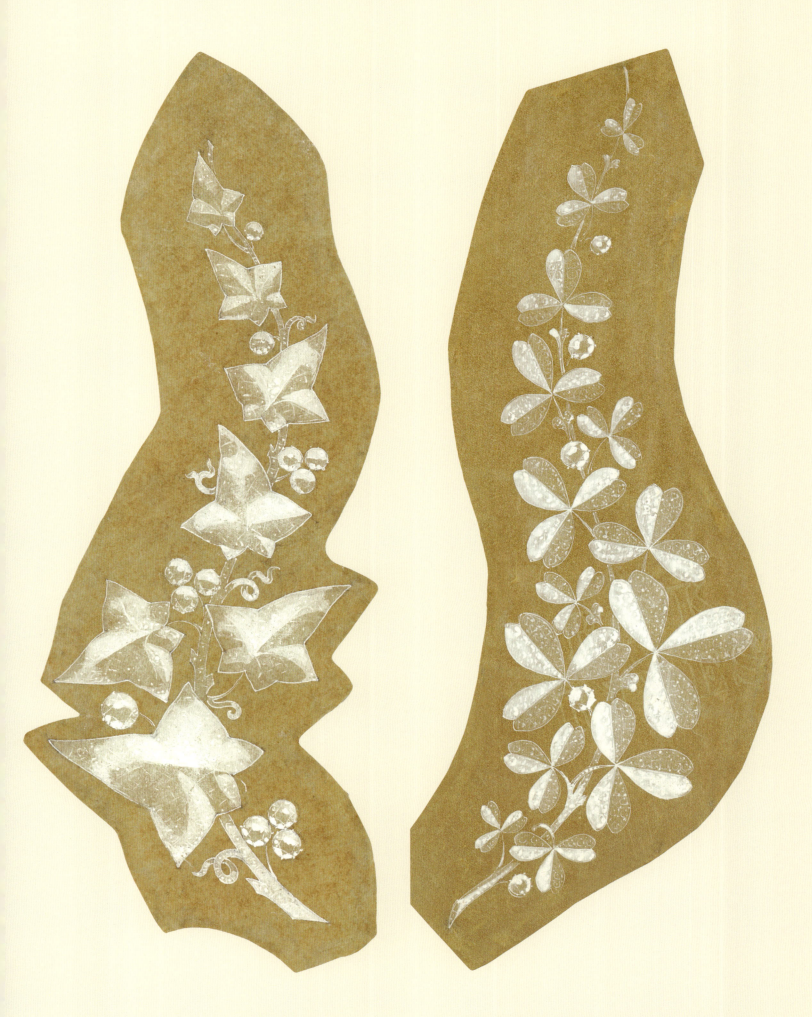

Design for an ivy corsage brooch, Joseph Chaumet, drawing studio, c. 1890, gouache and wash on translucent paper.

Design for a clover corsage brooch, Joseph Chaumet, drawing studio, c. 1900, gouache and wash on translucent paper.

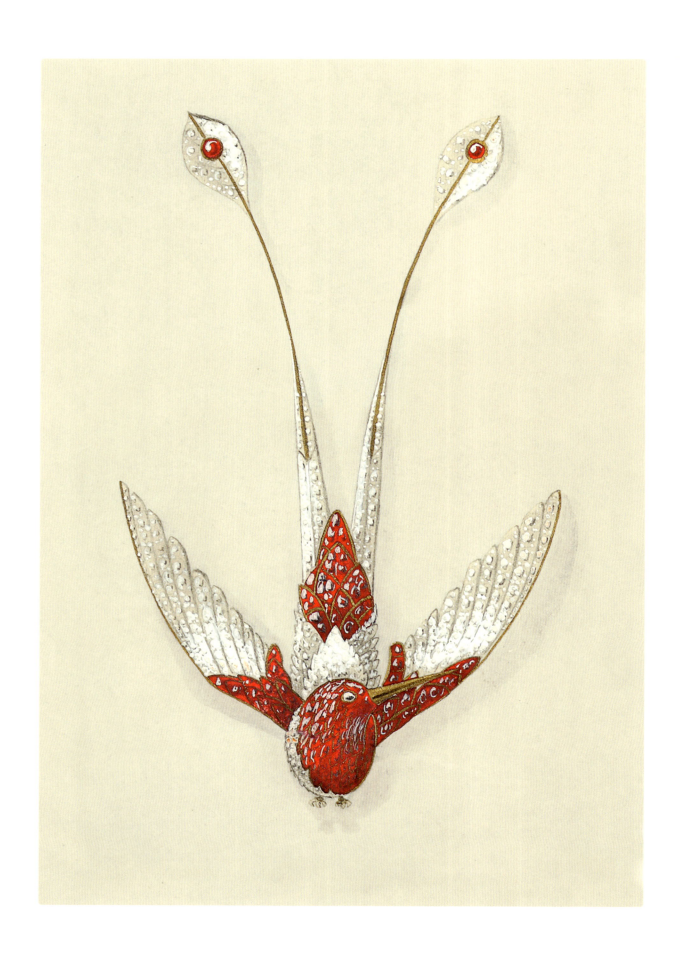

Bestiary

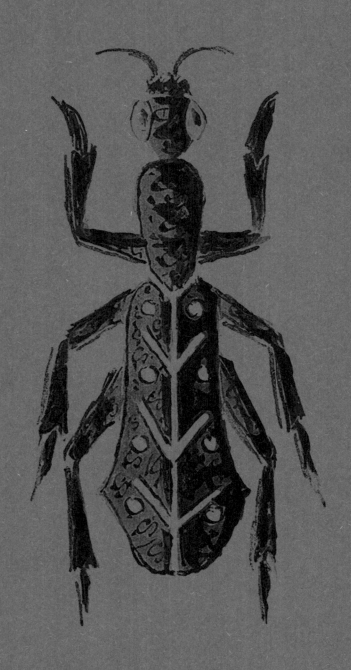

Above Design for an insect brooch, Joseph Chaumet,
drawing studio, c. 1880, graphite pencil, gouache, wash
and gold pigment on tinted paper.

Page 144 Design for a hummingbird brooch, Joseph Chaumet,
drawing studio, c. 1880, graphite pencil, gouache,
wash and gold pigment on tinted paper.

Bestiary

Jewellery and the decorative arts have looked to animals – real and imaginary, wild and domesticated, winged and aquatic – as a source of inspiration. Although the major classifications of the animal kingdom were established in the 17th and 18th centuries, it was only in the 19th century that animal motifs began to attract jewellers, on account of their expressiveness and symbolic weight. Among Maison Chaumet's designs is a bestiary covering a wide range of animal figures, with birds, butterflies and snakes appearing most frequently. Napoléon chose the eagle of ancient Rome and the bee of the Emperor Charlemagne as the emblems of his budding empire, while the Empress Joséphine was attracted by the dove, the swan and the butterfly (animals associated with Venus and love). These creatures, newly elevated to the rank of imperial symbols, thus formed part of the elaborate commissions delivered by Marie-Étienne Nitot. By the second half of the 19th century, bird motifs formed a mainstay of jewellery design. Easier travel provided greater opportunities to observe all types of exotic birds, and this growing enthusiasm was given extra impetus by the findings of the French naturalists Georges Cuvier and Alcide d'Orbigny. One result was a fashion for 'bird paradises' and 'bird bushes'.[2] Chaumet's jewellers took advantage of the diversity of shapes, lines, colours and poses offered by bird subjects. Producing work similar to that of animal artists, Jules Fossin produced a strikingly realistic, almost scientific series of birds' heads and legs that demonstrated the link between art and science. By the end of the 19th century, however, anatomical exactitude had given way to a more innovative approach. Joseph Chaumet's hummingbird aigrette, from 1880, used feathers as a defining metaphor for the lightness of flight. Chaumet's designs for winged tiaras also met with great success. Later on, Pierre Sterlé, an avant-garde jeweller working in the second half of the 20th century, would follow the example of his friend Georges Braque by trying to capture the essence of a bird's flight using simplified lines bordering on abstraction. Insects were also subjected to the miniaturising treatment and refined sensibility of jewellery design. The butterfly in particular has for centuries symbolised metamorphosis and transient beauty. During the First Empire in France, it represented love, before becoming one of the favorite insects of Art Nouveau, where it was associated with female figures or hidden among foliage in *trompe-l'oeil* designs. Joseph Chaumet's stylised butterflies, reminiscent of Odilon Redon's Symbolist watercolours, evoked the fragility and ephemerality of nature. On an edgier note, the shape and ancestral symbolism associated with snakes also made them perfect decorative elements for jewellery, since they could be made to coil around a wrist or slide down a cleavage. Other wild animals crop up occasionally in the Chaumet bestiary, alongside domesticated animals, particularly on clips from the 1960s and 1970s. The Maison's curiosity about the animal world thus seems boundless. Its daring spirit is especially evident in its wondrous vision of nature, which embraces everything from unsettling imaginary creatures – a griffin with an eagle's body, a lion's hindquarters and a horse's ears – to sea animals such as octopuses, starfish and seahorses.

Bestiary

Opposite, above Design for an eagle corsage brooch, Joseph Chaumet, drawing studio, c. 1890, gouache and wash on tinted paper.

Opposite, below Design for a butterfly corsage brooch, Joseph Chaumet, drawing studio, c. 1890, gouache and wash on tinted paper.

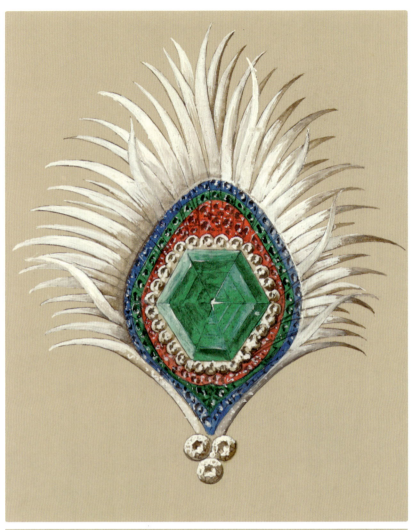

Top Design for a peacock-feather aigrette, Prosper Morel, drawing studio, *c.* 1870, graphite pencil, grey ink, gouache and brown ink wash on tinted paper.

Left Design for a peacock-feather aigrette, Prosper Morel, drawing studio, *c.* 1870, graphite pencil, grey ink, gouache, ink wash and gum arabic on tinted paper.

Opposite Design for a peacock corsage brooch, Joseph Chaumet, drawing studio, *c.* 1890, pen and black ink, gouache and ink wash with gold pigment on tinted paper.

A bird that glitters like
a jewel case,
Whose iridescent neck
reflects the rainbow !

Alphonse de Lamartine, 'Sur une plage', 1849

Design for a peacock-feather tiara, Joseph Chaumet, drawing studio,
c. 1915, graphite pencil, gouache and wash on tinted paper.

Above Design for a feather aigrette,
Joseph Chaumet, drawing studio,
c. 1900, gouache and wash
on tinted paper.

Right Design for a peacock aigrette,
Joseph Chaumet, drawing studio,
c. 1900, gouache and wash
on tinted paper.

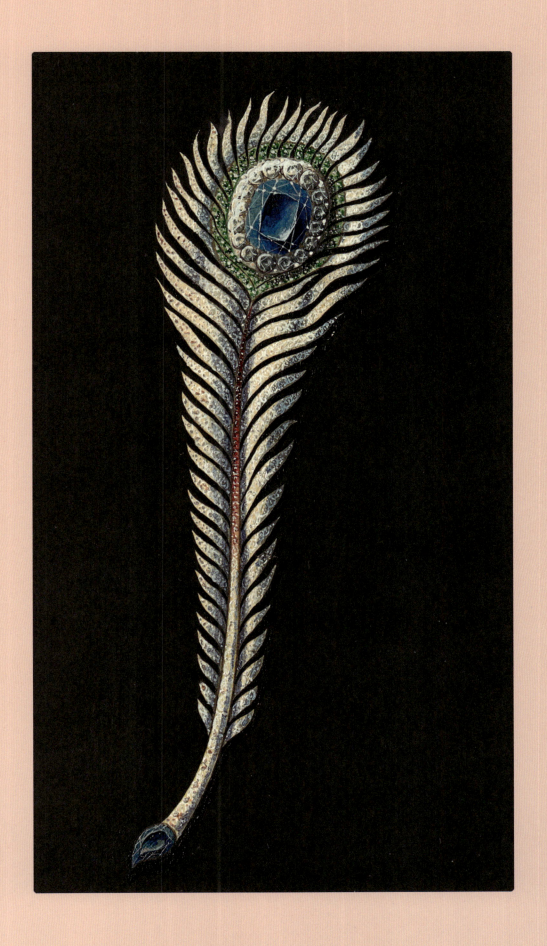

Design for a peacock-feather brooch,
Prosper Morel, drawing studio, c. 1870, gouache
and wash with gum arabic on tinted paper.

Previous pages Design for a peacock-feather necklace, Joseph Chaumet,
drawing studio, c. 1900–15, gouache and wash on tinted paper.

Above Design for a tiara with feather motifs, Joseph Chaumet, drawing studio,
c. 1900–10, graphite pencil, gouache and wash on tinted paper.

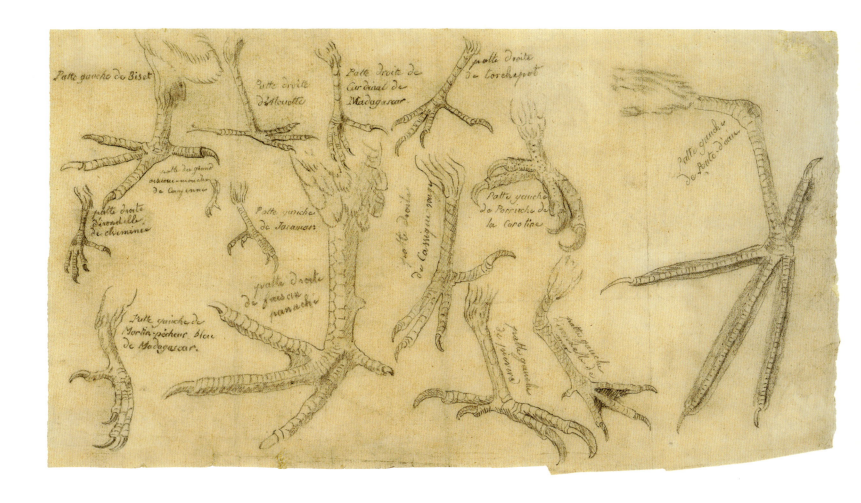

Birds' Heads and Feet

Chaumet's graphic artists studied birds with all the dedication of ornithologists, homing in on details such as beaks, eyes, scaly legs, talons and stunning plumage. Indeed, the precision of their notes, which record the species' vernacular names, their scientific genus or the different types of claws, reveal a deep understanding of ornithology. It is surprising to come across this degree of scientific accuracy in the archives of a jewellery house. The meticulous attention to detail, as well as the diversity of the species that are represented, suggests that Chaumet's draughtsmen very probably consulted natural history collections as part of their research. Their choice of birds was extremely eclectic, ranging from the wood nuthatch, found in European woodlands, to the Mascarene martin, which is native to Madagascar. Touchingly, these drawings sometimes even bear witness to birds that are now extinct: one sheet of drawings shows, in the centre, the left leg of a Carolina parakeet – a species from the south-eastern United States that was wiped out in the early 20th century. · MARC JEANSON

Above Studies of birds' feet, Jules Fossin, drawing studio,
c. 1840, graphite pencil on translucent paper.

tête d'écorcheur mâle

tête à bec-croisé mâle

tête d'hirondelle de cheminée

tête de cardinal de madagascar

tête d'étourneau

tête de gobe mouche à longue queue de madagascar

tête de proyer

tête de rossignol de muraille mâle

tête de niguu-bœuf

Tête de torchepot.

tête de bouvreuil mâle

tête de tangara verd du pérou

tête du grand oiseau mouche de Cayenne

Studies of birds' heads, Jules Fossin, drawing studio,
c. 1840, graphite pencil on translucent paper.

Come, let yourself delight in these wings of fire!

Alphonse de Lamartine, 'Dieu', 1830

Above Winged aigrette with diamonds and blue
enamel, Joseph Chaumet, photography lab, 1905,
silver gelatin print from glass plate negative.

Top Design for a winged aigrette, Joseph Chaumet, drawing studio, c. 1900–10, graphite pencil, grey ink, gouache and wash on tinted paper.

Above Design for a winged aigrette, Joseph Chaumet, drawing studio, c. 1900, graphite pencil, gouache and wash on tinted paper.

Top Design for a winged aigrette, Joseph Chaumet, drawing studio, *c.* 1900, graphite pencil, gouache and wash on translucent paper.

Above Design for a winged aigrette, Joseph Chaumet, drawing studio, *c.* 1900–10, graphite pencil, gouache and wash on translucent paper.

Two designs for winged aigrettes, Joseph Chaumet,
drawing studio, *c.* 1900, graphite pencil, gouache
and wash on translucent paper.

Then the sky fills
with a million
swallows (...)
From Africa come
the ibis, the flamingo,
the marabou stork (...)
And from America comes
the little hummingbird.

Guillaume Apollinaire, 'Zone', 1913

Top Winged tiara made for Mrs. Payne Whitney,
née Gertrude Vanderbilt, Joseph Chaumet, 1910,
platinum, diamonds and enamel.

Above Design for a winged tiara for
Mrs. Payne Whitney, Joseph Chaumet, drawing
studio, 1910, graphite pencil, pen and grey ink
with gouache wash on tinted paper.

Opposite, above Design for a
winged aigrette, Joseph Chaumet,
drawing studio, c. 1900, graphite pencil,
grey ink, gouache and wash on
tinted paper.

Opposite, below Design
for a winged corsage brooch,
Joseph Chaumet, drawing studio,
c. 1900, graphite pencil, gouache
and wash on tinted paper.

Above Winged aigrette,
Joseph Chaumet, photography lab,
c. 1890–1900, silver gelatin print
from glass plate negative.

The splendid eagle that dwells amid the thunder
Takes wing; and from his audacious flight,
Seems to say to mortals: I was born on the earth,
But I live in the skies.

Alphonse de Lamartine, 'La gloire', 1820

Above Design for a winged aigrette with ribbons, Joseph Chaumet,
drawing studio, *c.* 1900, gouache and wash on translucent paper.

Design for an eagle aigrette with fleur-de-lis, Joseph Chaumet,
drawing studio, c. 1890, gouache and brown ink wash on translucent paper.

Opposite Two designs for winged aigrettes,
Joseph Chaumet, drawing studio, c. 1900, graphite
pencil, gouache and wash on translucent paper.

Above Winged aigrette with leaves and *fil couteau*
setting, Joseph Chaumet, photography lab, c. 1890–1900,
silver gelatin print from glass plate negative.

Above Design for a tiara, Joseph Chaumet,
drawing studio, 1900–10, graphite pencil, gouache
and wash on tinted paper.

Opposite Design for a winged tiara,
Joseph Chaumet, drawing studio, 1900–10, graphite
pencil, gouache and wash on tinted paper.

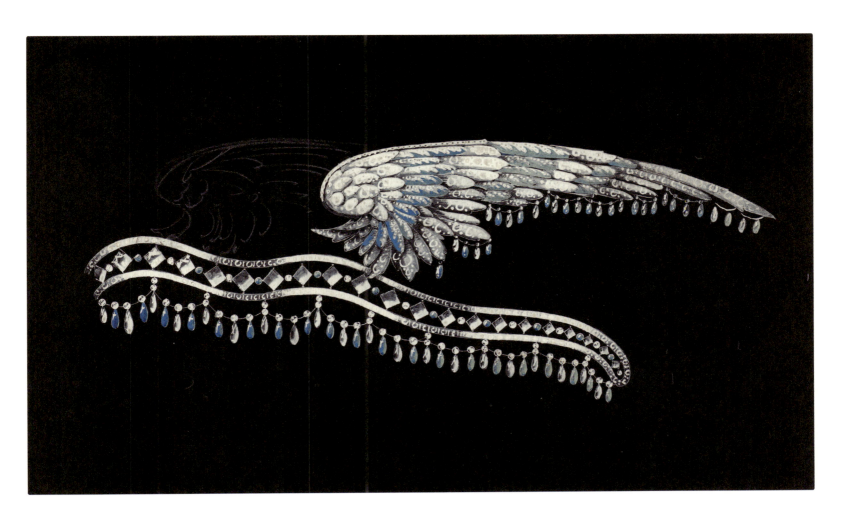

But all the jewels of ancient Palmyra,
The unknown metals, the pearls of the sea,
Set by your hand, could never match
That lovely diadem, dazzling and bright.

Charles Baudelaire, 'Bénédiction', 1857

Above Design for a winged aigrette, Joseph Chaumet, drawing studio, 1900–10, graphite pencil, gouache and wash on translucent paper.

Right Design for a lion-head brooch with wings, Joseph Chaumet, drawing studio, 1900–10, graphite pencil, gouache and wash on translucent paper.

Opposite Design for a winged necklace with looping chain, Joseph Chaumet, drawing studio, c. 1900, graphite pencil, gouache and wash on translucent paper.

Three designs for a lizard corsage brooch for Princess Katharina Henckel von Donnersmarck,
Joseph Chaumet, drawing studio, 1889, graphite pencil, gouache and wash on translucent paper.

Designs for snake cuff bracelets, Joseph Chaumet, drawing
studio, 1880–90, gouache and wash on tinted paper.

To see you move in rhythm,
beautiful in your abandon,
Brings to mind a dancing serpent,
coiled around a cane.

Charles Baudelaire, 'Le serpent qui danse', 1857

Above Design for a choker with snakes and leaves, Joseph Chaumet,
drawing studio, *c.* 1900, gouache and wash on tinted paper.

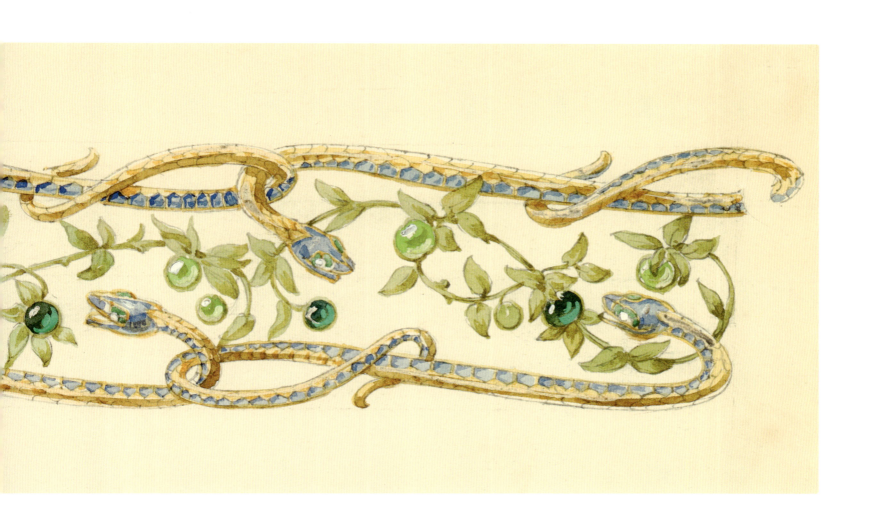

Design for a tiara with confronted snakes, Joseph Chaumet, drawing studio,
c. 1890–1900, pen and black ink, graphite pencil, gouache and wash on tinted paper.

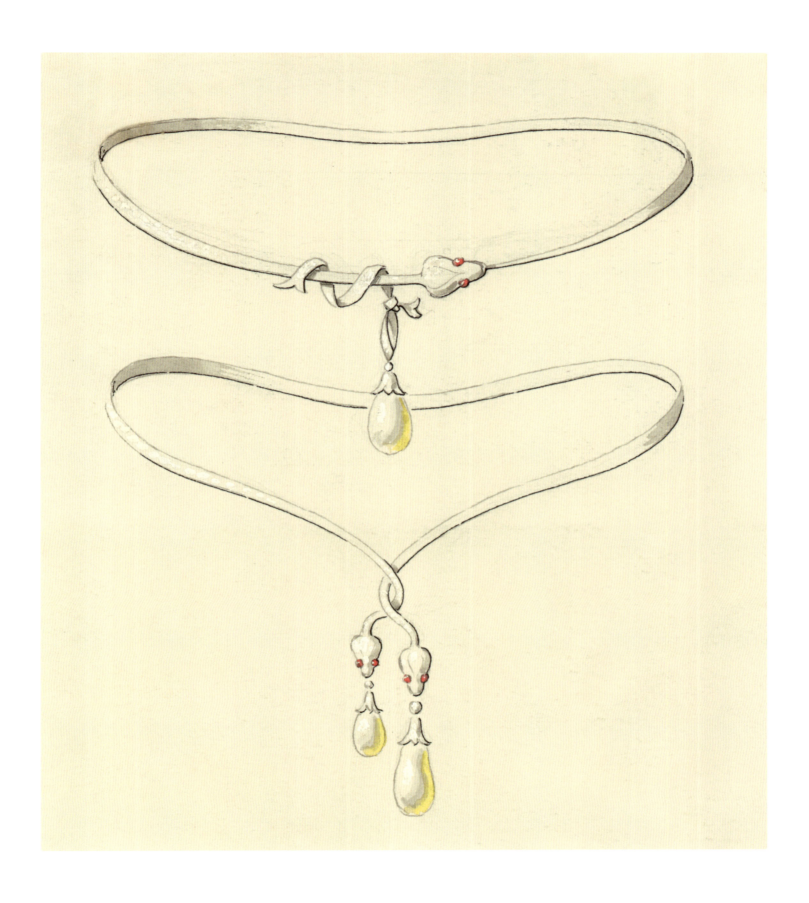

Opposite Design for a twisted snake necklace,
Joseph Chaumet, drawing studio, 1880-90, graphite
pencil, gouache and wash on tinted paper.

Above Two designs for snake necklaces with pendent
pearls, Joseph Chaumet, drawing studio, *c.* 1900, graphite
pencil, gouache and wash on tinted paper.

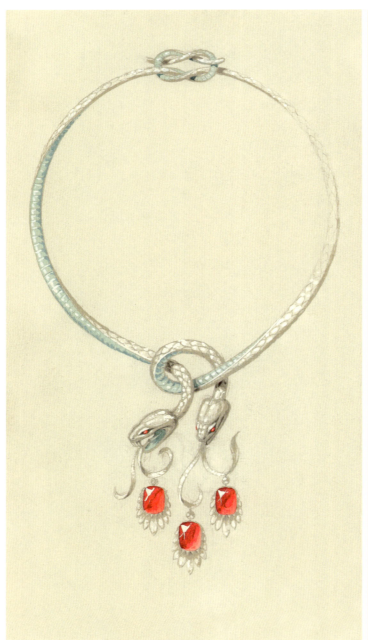

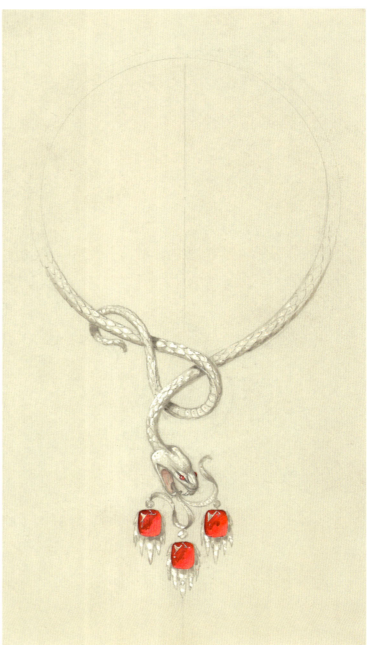

Above left Design for a necklace with entwined snakes,
Joseph Chaumet, drawing studio, c. 1900, graphite
pencil, gouache and wash on tinted paper.

Above right Design for a necklace with twisted snake,
Joseph Chaumet, drawing studio, c. 1900, graphite
pencil, gouache and wash on tinted paper.

Opposite Two designs for brittlestar shoulder
ornaments, Joseph Chaumet, drawing studio, c. 1900,
graphite pencil, pen and ink, ink wash and
watercolour on tinted paper.

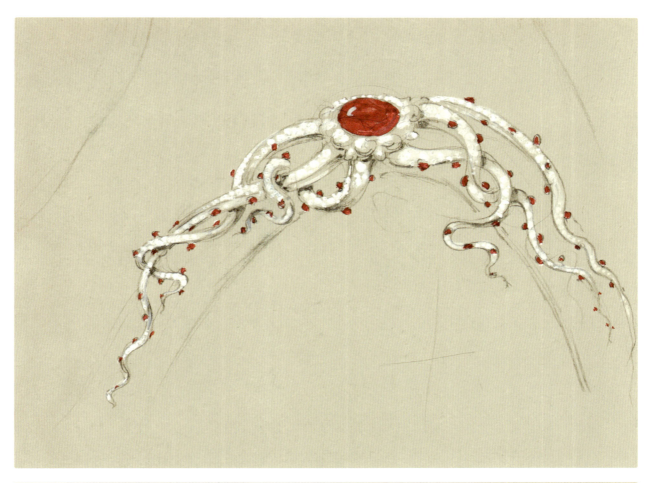

Designs for a series of parrot brooches, Joseph Chaumet, drawing studio,
c. 1910, graphite pencil, gouache and wash on tinted paper.

Designs for a series of frog, lizard and tortoise brooches, Joseph Chaumet, drawing studio,
c. 1910, graphite pencil, gouache and wash on tinted paper.

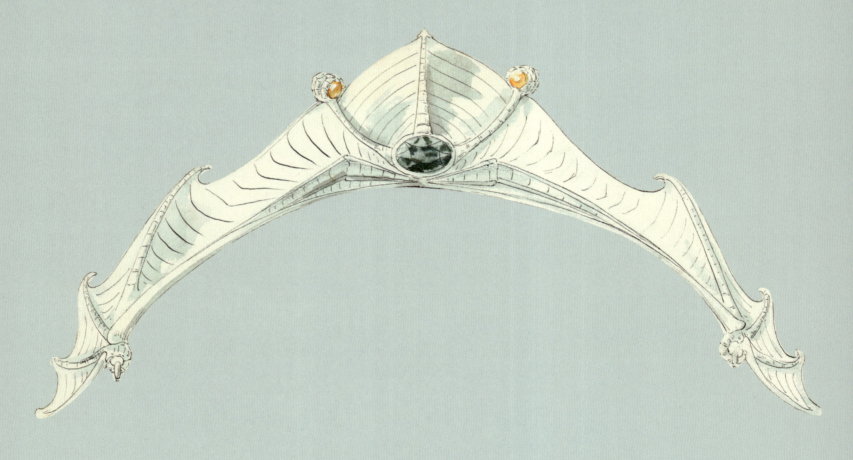

Top Design for a bat-wing tiara, Joseph Chaumet, drawing studio, c. 1900–10, graphite pencil, gouache and wash on tinted paper.

Above Design for a bat-wing tiara, Joseph Chaumet, drawing studio, 1900–10, graphite pencil, gouache and ink wash on tinted paper.

Design for a clock with a mouse nibbling
a sugar cube, René Morin, drawing studio, 1978,
gouache and wash on tinted paper.

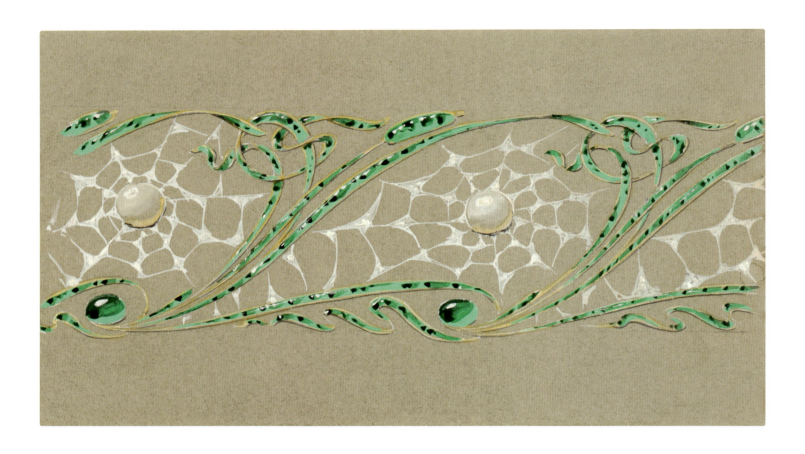

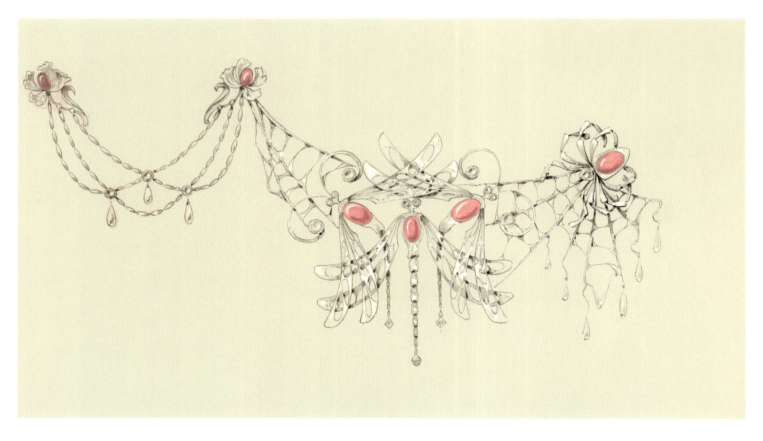

Top Design for a spiderweb choker,
Joseph Chaumet, drawing studio, C. 1900,
gouache and wash on tinted paper.

Above Design for a corsage brooch with dragonflies,
spider and flowers, Joseph Chaumet, drawing studio,
C. 1900–10, graphite pencil, pen and grey ink,
gouache and ink wash on tinted paper.

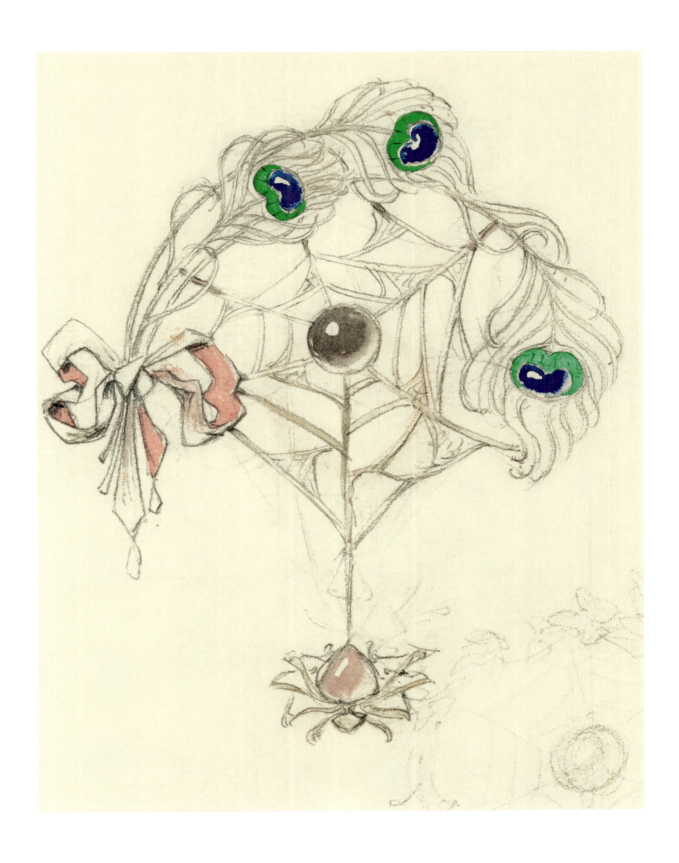

Design for a brooch with spiderweb, spider, bow
and peacock-feather motifs, Joseph Chaumet, drawing
studio, c. 1900, graphite pencil, gouache and
wash on tinted paper.

Like a fan of silk,
It unfolds
Its cloak, glittering with silver;
And its rainbow gown
Is gilded
With shifting hues of gold.

Gérard de Nerval, 'Les papillons', 1832

Opposite Design for a stylised butterfly aigrette, Joseph Chaumet, drawing studio, c. 1910, graphite pencil, gouache and wash on tinted paper.

Top Design for a butterfly brooch that transforms into an aigrette, Joseph Chaumet, drawing studio, c. 1890, gouache and wash with gold pigment on translucent paper.

Above Design for a butterfly aigrette that transforms into a brooch, Joseph Chaumet, drawing studio, c. 1890, graphite pencil, gouache and wash on translucent paper.

Above Design for a winged aigrette,
Joseph Chaumet, drawing studio, *c.* 1900, graphite
pencil, gouache and wash on tinted paper.

Opposite Design for a dragonfly brooch,
Joseph Chaumet, drawing studio, 1900–10, graphite
pencil, gouache and wash on tinted paper.

Around them swirl in flight
Love, illusion, hope,
Like Flora's insect beloved,
Whose wings seem to bloom
With late evening light.

Alphonse de Lamartine, 'Adieux à la poésie', 1860

Top Design for a floral tiara with two birds
and a fountain, Joseph Chaumet, drawing studio,
1910–20, graphite pencil, gouache and
wash on tinted paper.

Above Design for a Persian-inspired tiara
with winged lions, Joseph Chaumet, drawing
studio, 1910–20, graphite pencil, gouache
and wash on tinted paper.

Two designs for Egyptian-inspired corsage brooches,
c. 1920, Marcel Chaumet, drawing studio, graphite pencil
and gouache on tinted paper.

A swan's neck
that curves,
As supple as
a branch
Caressed by a cool
evening breeze

Théophile Gautier, 'Cher ange, vous êtes belle', 1830

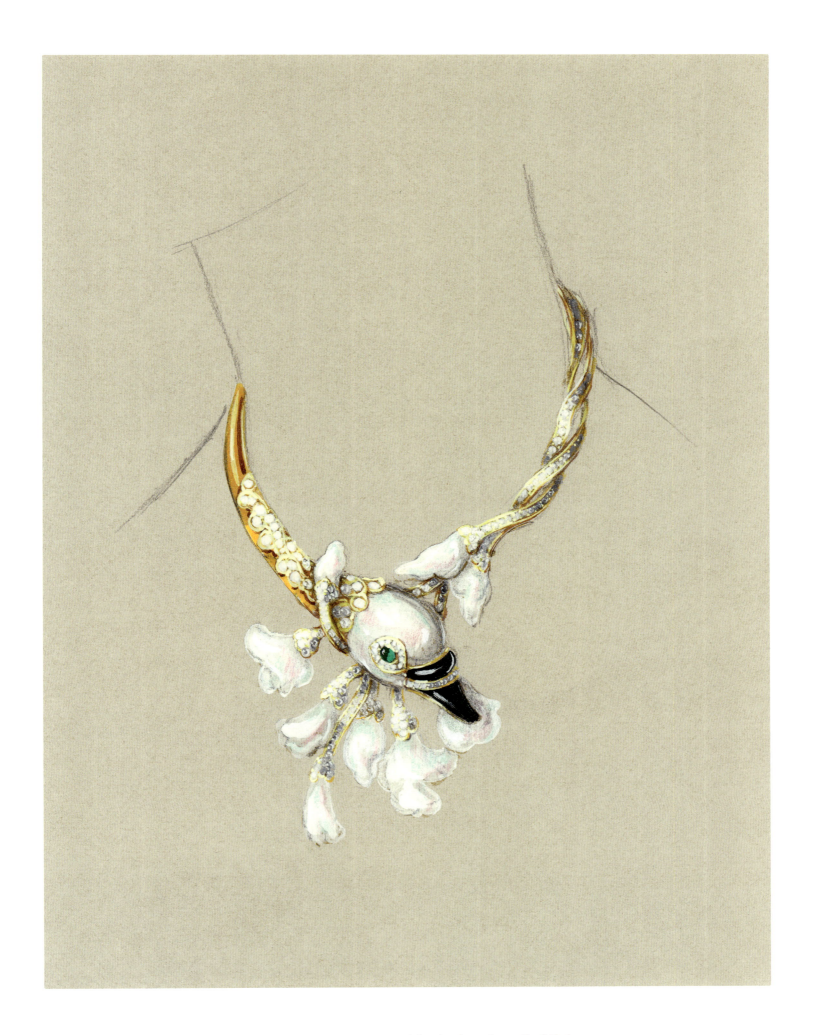

Design for a torc necklace with swan's head and sweet peas, René Morin,
drawing studio, c. 1981, graphite pencil, gouache and wash on tracing paper.

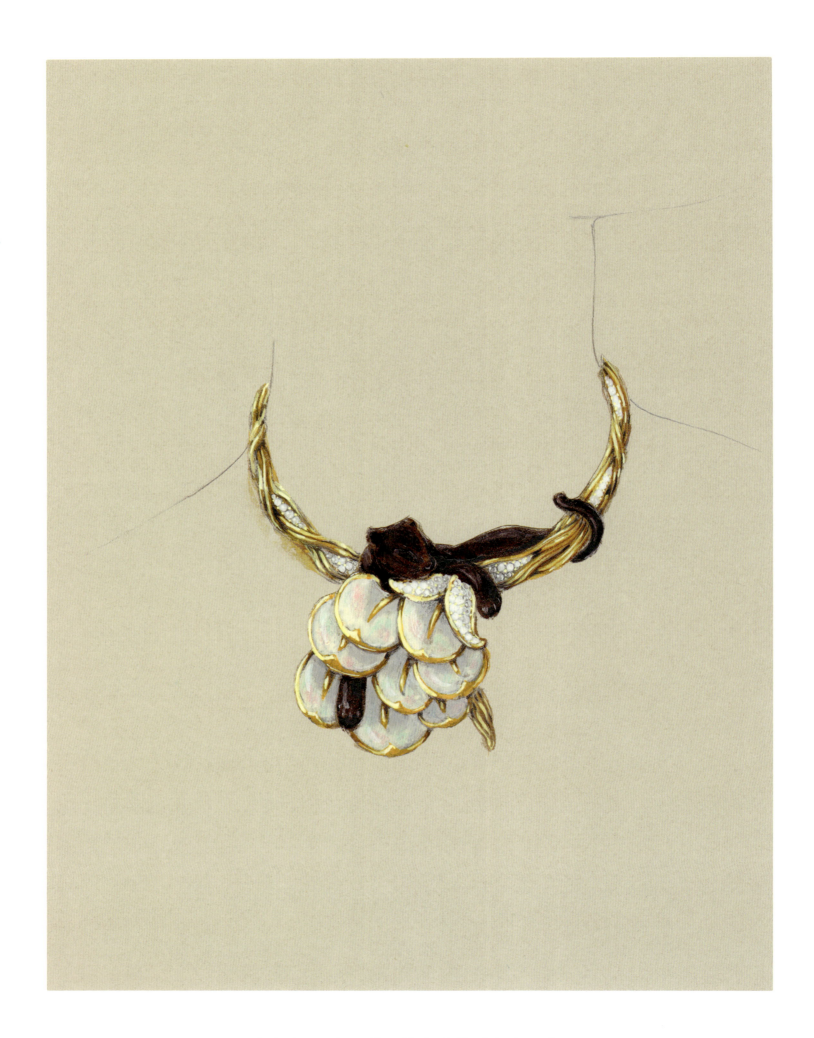

Design for a panther necklace, Béatrice de Plinval, drawing studio,
c. 1981, graphite pencil, gouache and wash on tracing paper.

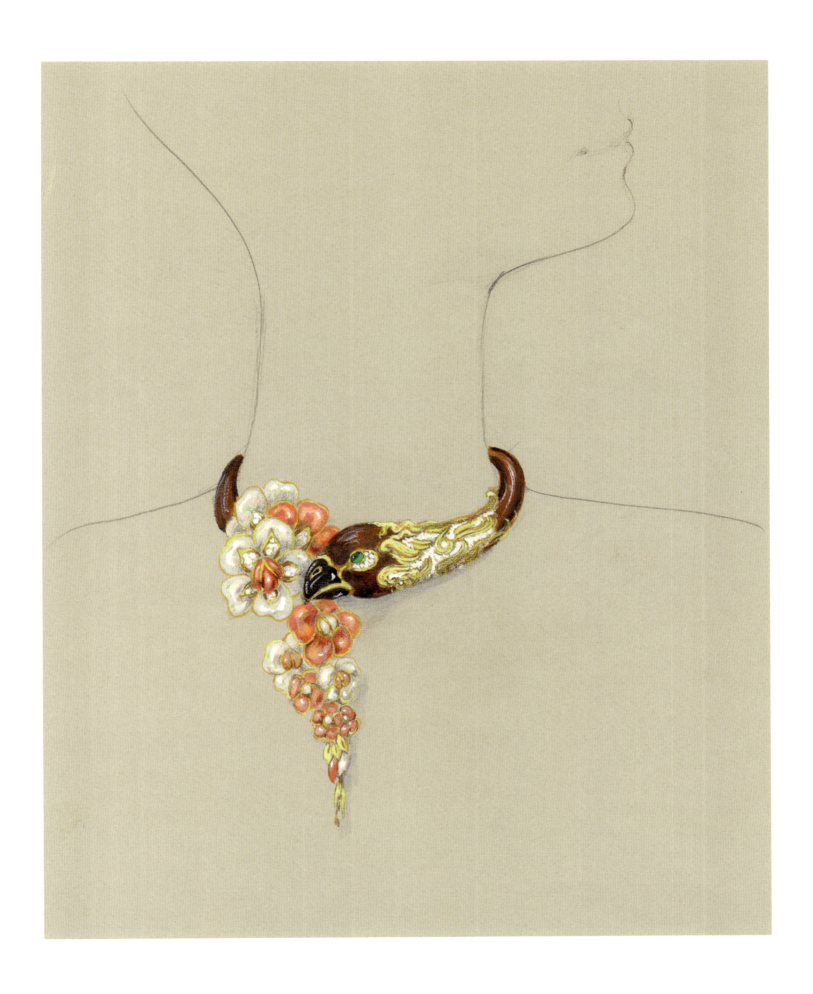

Design for a parrot necklace with floral spray, René Morin, drawing studio,
c. 1980, graphite pencil, gouache and wash on tracing paper.

Above left Design for a ram's head brooch,
Gisèle Crevier, drawing studio, 1965–70,
gouache and wash on tracing paper.

Above right Design for a brooch with two
birds on a branch, Gisèle Crevier, drawing studio,
1965–70, gouache and wash on tracing paper.

Right Design for an owl brooch,
Gisèle Crevier, drawing studio, 1969, gouache
and wash on tracing paper.

Opposite Design for a peacock necklace,
Gisèle Crevier, drawing studio, 1965–70, gouache
and wash on tracing paper.

Above Design for a hummingbird aigrette,
Joseph Chaumet, drawing studio, c. 1880,
gouache, wash, gold pigment and
gum arabic on tinted paper.

Opposite Hummingbird aigrette,
Joseph Chaumet, c. 1880, gold, silver,
rubies and diamonds.

Universe

Above Designs for sunburst aigrette and corsage brooch
with interlaced crescent moons, Joseph Chaumet, drawing studio,
1900–15, graphite pencil, gouache and wash on tinted paper.

Page 206 Design for a starburst aigrette, Joseph Chaumet, drawing studio,
c. 1900, gouache, wash, gold pigment and gum arabic on translucent paper.

Universe

'It is sweet to observe the glowing star, a speck
of gold embroidered on the canopy of the firmament.'[3]

This line by the celebrated Romantic poet Théophile Gautier, evoking the starry sky as an object of wonder, reveals the 19th-century fascination with the vastness of the universe and the scientific origin of the heavenly bodies. As the century advanced, intellectuals gradually assimilated the notion of a boundless cosmos that would no longer induce fear or vertigo. Chaumet's jewellers reflected the tastes of their times by drawing inspiration from the infinite nature of skies, clouds and stars. During the Second Empire, astronomical themes began to appear on countless designs for stomachers, tiaras and aigrettes, mainly in the form of crescent moons, suns, stars and, less commonly, rainbows. This iconography was evidence of our better understanding of the atmospheric and optical phenomena that have always featured in art. The sky – a favourite subject of painters such as Pierre-Henri de Valenciennes, J. M. W. Turner and Eugène Boudin – became a major field of research into the relationship between matter, light and atmosphere. Joseph Chaumet turned his attention away from stars and crescent moons and focused on the sun motif, with its beams radiating from a large diamond or coloured stone set in the centre of a jewel. The impressive sun tiara commissioned by the wealthy aristocrat William George Cavendish-Bentinck in 1906 conveyed the power of the solar disc by creating the impression of light constantly gushing forth. This design, imbued with a dynamism typical of Art Deco, was considered extremely modern at the time. During the Belle Époque, the motifs of water rising and falling, of waves and frozen stalactites, also entered the repertoire, derived from natural phenomena. Designs for jewels worn on the head, such as 'waterfall' aigrettes and tiaras, demonstrated the degree of precision that was possible in this ceaselessly honed technique: there was a trend towards increasingly dainty mounts that resulted in an unprecedented degree of refinement and poetry. The themes of air and water, first developed at the turn of the 19th century as part of an aesthetic of the Sublime, still inspire the Maison's collections today. Chaumet's dazzling, dream-like representation of the universe in jewellery, drawing on both Romantic lyricism and scientific rigour, has found a contemporary-counterpart in our era's new sensitivity to nature.

189

Each ray of moonlight is a stream of honey

Guillaume Apollinaire, 'Clair de Lune', 1913

Opposite Aigrette with crescent moon
and star, Joseph Chaumet, photography lab,
c. 1890–1900, silver gelatin print from
glass plate negative.

Above Design for an aigrette with
crescent moon and stars, Joseph Chaumet,
drawing studio, c. 1900–15, graphite pencil,
gouache and wash on tinted paper.

Above Design for an aigrette with interlaced crescent moons, Joseph Chaumet, drawing studio, *c.* 1900–15, gouache and wash on translucent paper.

Right Design for an openwork crescent-moon aigrette, Joseph Chaumet, drawing studio, *c.* 1900–15, graphite pencil, gouache and wash on translucent paper.

Opposite Two designs for crescent-moon aigrettes, Joseph Chaumet, drawing studio, *c.* 1900–15, graphite pencil, gouache and wash on translucent paper.

The heavens are copper
With no glimmer of light,
It seems we could watch
the moon live and die.

Paul Verlaine, 'Dans l'interminable...', 1874

Above Design for a crescent-moon aigrette, Joseph Chaumet, drawing studio, c. 1900–15, graphite pencil, gouache and wash on tinted paper.

Opposite, above Design for an aigrette with three crescent moons, Joseph Chaumet, drawing studio, 1909, graphite pencil, gouache and wash on tinted paper.

Opposite, below Design for a crescent-moon corsage brooch, Joseph Chaumet, drawing studio, c. 1910–15, graphite pencil, gouache and wash on tinted paper.

Opposite, above Design for a stalagmite tiara, Chaumet, drawing studio, c. 1910–15, graphite pencil, gouache and wash on tinted paper.

Opposite, below Designs for brooches with interlaced crescent moons, Joseph Chaumet, drawing studio, c. 1900–15, graphite pencil, gouache and wash on tinted paper.

Above Design for a crescent-moon aigrette, Joseph Chaumet. drawing studio, c. 1900–15, graphite pencil, gouache and wash on tinted paper.

The moon is in the sky
and the sky is unveiled (…)
From far away, it lights
the path of the stars
And their white trails
amid the ocean of blue.

Alphonse de Lamartine, 'Harmonies poétiques et religieuses', 1830

Opposite Design for an aigrette with interlaced crescent
moons, Chaumet, drawing studio, c. 1900–10, graphite
pencil, gouache and wash on tinted paper.

Above Design for a transformable necklace
with interlaced crescent moons and stars, Chaumet,
drawing studio, 1900–10, graphite pencil, gouache,
wash and gum arabic on tinted paper.

I have hung ropes from belltower to belltower;
Garlands from window to window;
Golden chains from star to star, and I dance.

Arthur Rimbaud, 'Les Illuminations', 1886

Design for a tiara with stars, Joseph Chaumet, drawing studio, c. 1900,
graphite pencil, gouache and wash on tinted paper.

Top Tiara with stars, Joseph Chaumet, photography lab, 1909, silver gelatin print from glass plate negative.

Above Tiara with stars, Joseph Chaumet, photography lab, c. 1890–1900, silver gelatin print from glass plate negative.

Two designs for star aigrettes with *fil couteau* settings,
Joseph Chaumet, drawing studio, *c.* 1900–15, graphite
pencil, gouache and wash on tinted paper.

224

Five designs for star aigrettes, Joseph Chaumet, drawing studio, c. 1900–15, graphite pencil, gouache and wash on translucent paper.

The Great Bear
was my tavern.
My stars in the sky
whispered softly.

Arthur Rimbaud, 'Ma bohème', 1870

Design for a star tiara, Joseph Chaumet, drawing studio,
c. 1900–15, gouache and wash on tinted paper.

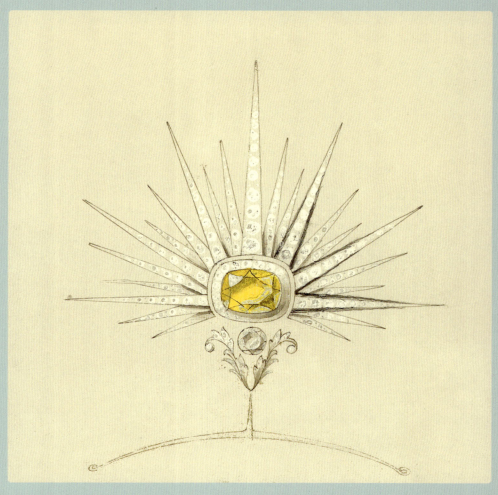

Above Design for a sunburst aigrette, Joseph Chaumet, drawing studio, *c.* 1900–15, graphite pencil, gouache and wash on tinted paper.

Right Design for a sunburst aigrette, Joseph Chaumet, drawing studio, *c.* 1900, graphite pencil, gouache and wash on tinted paper.

Opposite Design for a sunburst aigrette, Joseph Chaumet, drawing studio, *c.* 1910, graphite pencil, gouache and wash on tinted paper.

Show us the jewel case
of your richest memories,
Those wonderful gems,
made from stardust and ether.

Charles Baudelaire, 'Le voyage', 1857

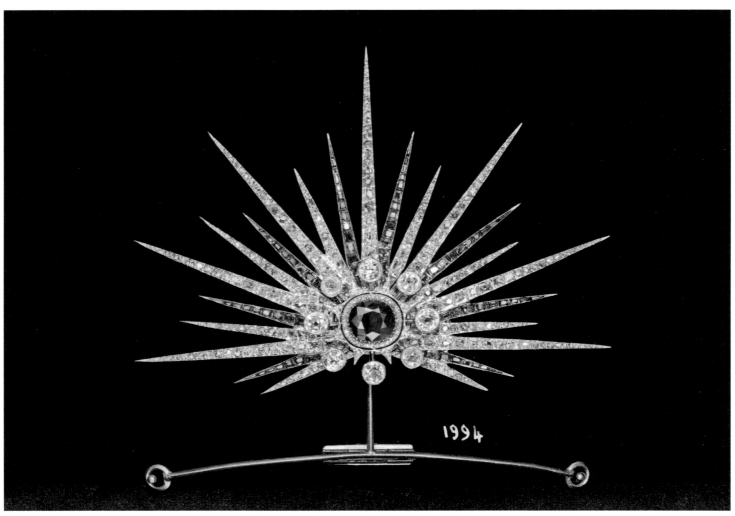

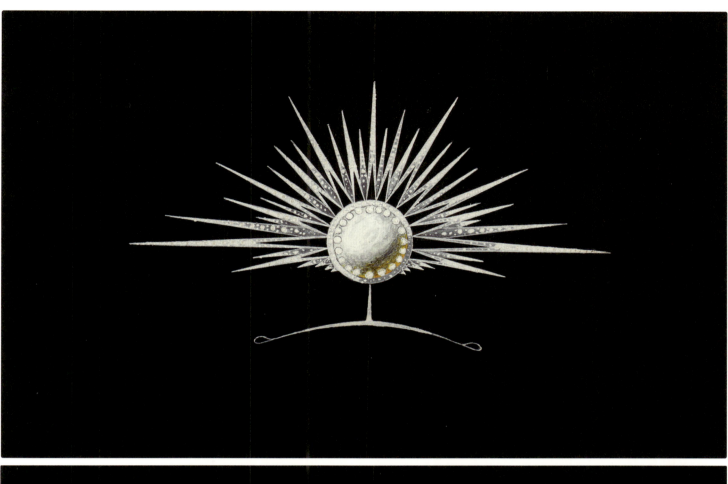

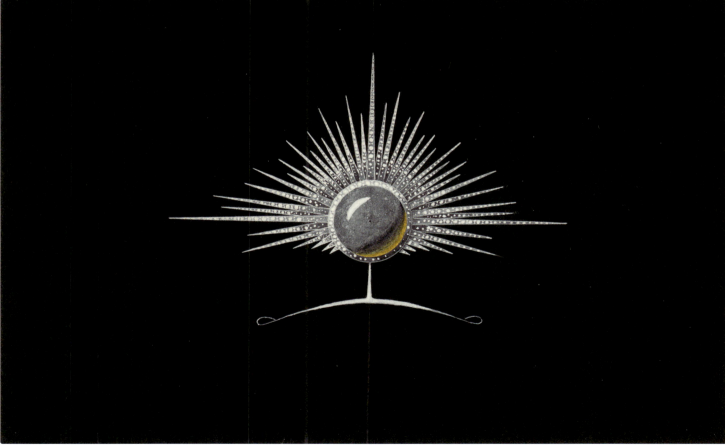

Opposite, below Sunburst aigrette, Joseph Chaumet,
photography lab, c. 1890–1900, silver gelatin print
from glass plate negative.

Above and opposite, above Designs for sunburst
aigrettes, Joseph Chaumet, drawing studio. c. 1910, graphite
pencil, gouache and wash on tinted paper.

Above Large sunburst tiara, Joseph Chaumet, photography lab, c. 1890–1900, silver gelatin print from glass plate negative.

Right Design for a sunburst aigrette, Joseph Chaumet, drawing studio, c. 1900–15, gouache and wash on translucent paper.

Opposite Two designs for a cloud necklace and pendant with baroque pearls, Joseph Chaumet, drawing studio, c. 1900–10, gouache and wash on tinted paper.

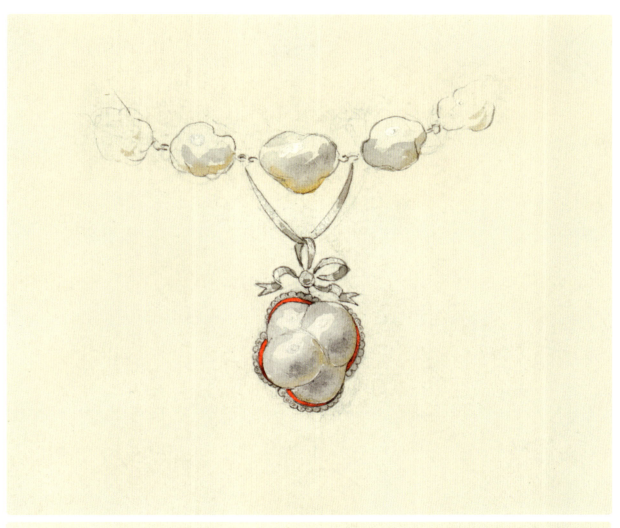

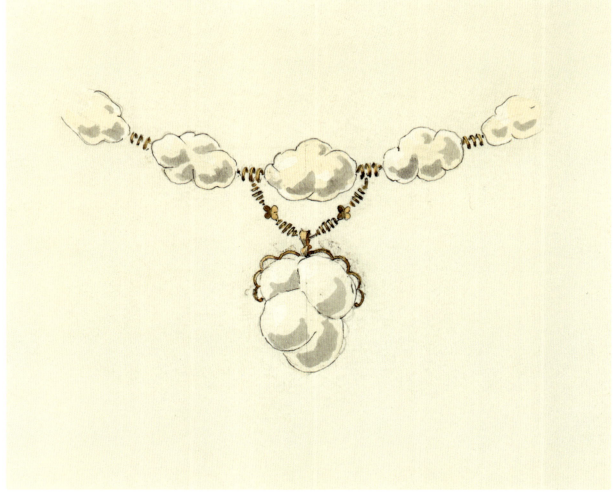

Design for an aigrette with flame motifs, Chaumet, drawing studio,
c. 1900, graphite pencil, gouache and ink wash on tinted paper.

Beautiful rainbow, emerge from the storm!

Victor Hugo, 'Il fait froid', 1856

Above Design for an aigrette with fountain and rainbow, Joseph Chaumet, drawing studio, c. 1900, graphite pencil, gouache and wash on tinted paper.

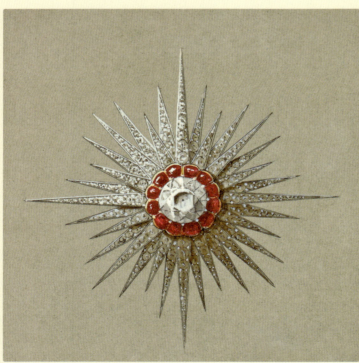
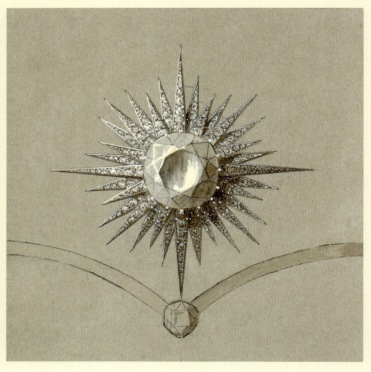

Designs for sunburst aigrettes, Joseph Chaumet, drawing studio,
c. 1900–15, ink, gouache, wash and gum arabic on tinted paper.

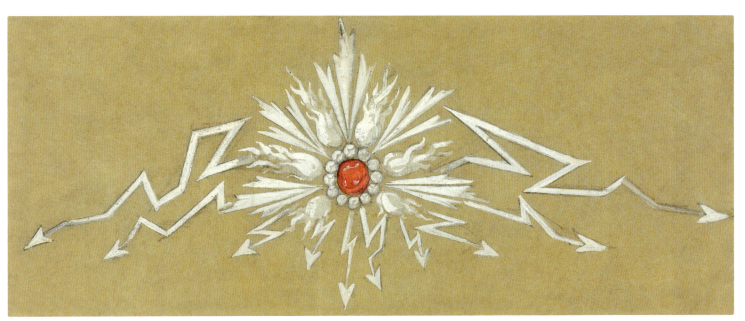

When shall we go to where the dawn and the thunder dwell?

Victor Hugo, 'Claire', 1856

Top Design for an aigrette with sun and clouds,
Joseph Chaumet, drawing studio, *c.* 1900, graphite
pencil, gouache and ink wash on tinted paper.

Above Design for a tiara with lightning bolts,
Joseph Chaumet, drawing studio, *c.* 1900, graphite
pencil, gouache and wash on translucent paper.

Above Sunburst tiara for the Princess Yusupov,
Joseph Chaumet, photography lab, 1913, silver
gelatin print from glass plate negative.

Opposite, above Design for an aigrette,
Joseph Chaumet, drawing studio, c. 1900–15,
gouache and wash on tinted paper.

Opposite, below Design for a corsage
brooch with sapphire starburst, Joseph Chaumet,
drawing studio, 1919, graphite pencil, gouache
and wash on tinted paper.

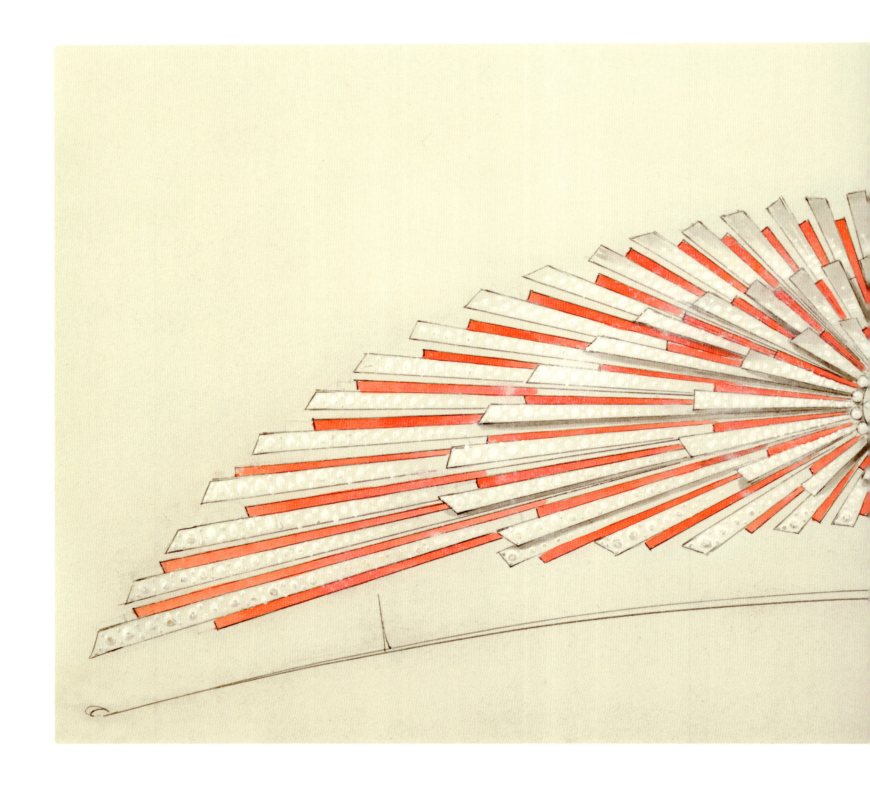

Roll along your pathways of flame,
You stars, kings of infinite space!

Alphonse de Lamartine, 'Éternité de la nature, brièveté de l'homme', 1830

Design for a tiara with three-layered sunburst, Joseph Chaumet, drawing studio,
c. 1910, graphite pencil, grey ink, gouache and ink wash on tinted paper.

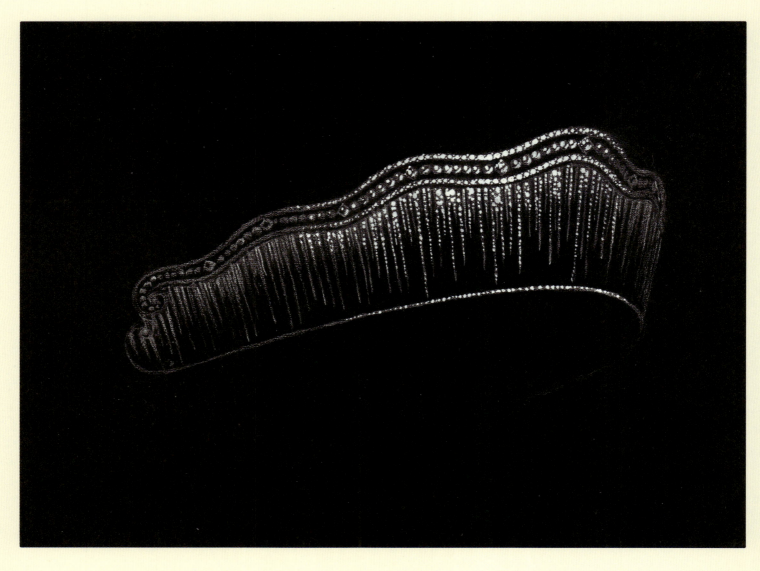

3305

Opposite, above Design for a tiara
with shooting stars, Joseph Chaumet,
drawing studio, *c.* 1900, graphite
pencil, gouache, wash and chalk
on tinted paper.

Opposite, below Design for
a stalactite tiara, Joseph Chaumet,
drawing studio, *c.* 1890–1900, graphite
pencil, gouache and wash on
tinted paper.

Above Stalactite tiara,
Joseph Chaumet, photography lab,
1904, silver gelatin print from glass
plate negative.

Time erases all, like the waves
on the flattened sand
Wash away the castles
built by children.
We shall forget these words,
so precise and yet so vague
Behind which each of us
senses infinity.

Marcel Proust, 'Je contemple souvent le ciel de ma mémoire'

Opposite Design for a wave tiara, Édouard Wibaille, drawing studio, 1889–1908, graphite pencil, gouache and wash on tinted paper.

Top Design for a tiara with volute motifs, Chaumet, drawing studio, c. 1950, graphite pencil, gouache and wash on tracing paper.

Above Design for a wave tiara, Joseph Chaumet, drawing studio, c. 1900, graphite pencil, gouache and wash on tinted paper.

Design for a seashell corsage brooch, Joseph Chaumet,
drawing studio, 1913, graphite pencil, gouache and wash on tinted paper.

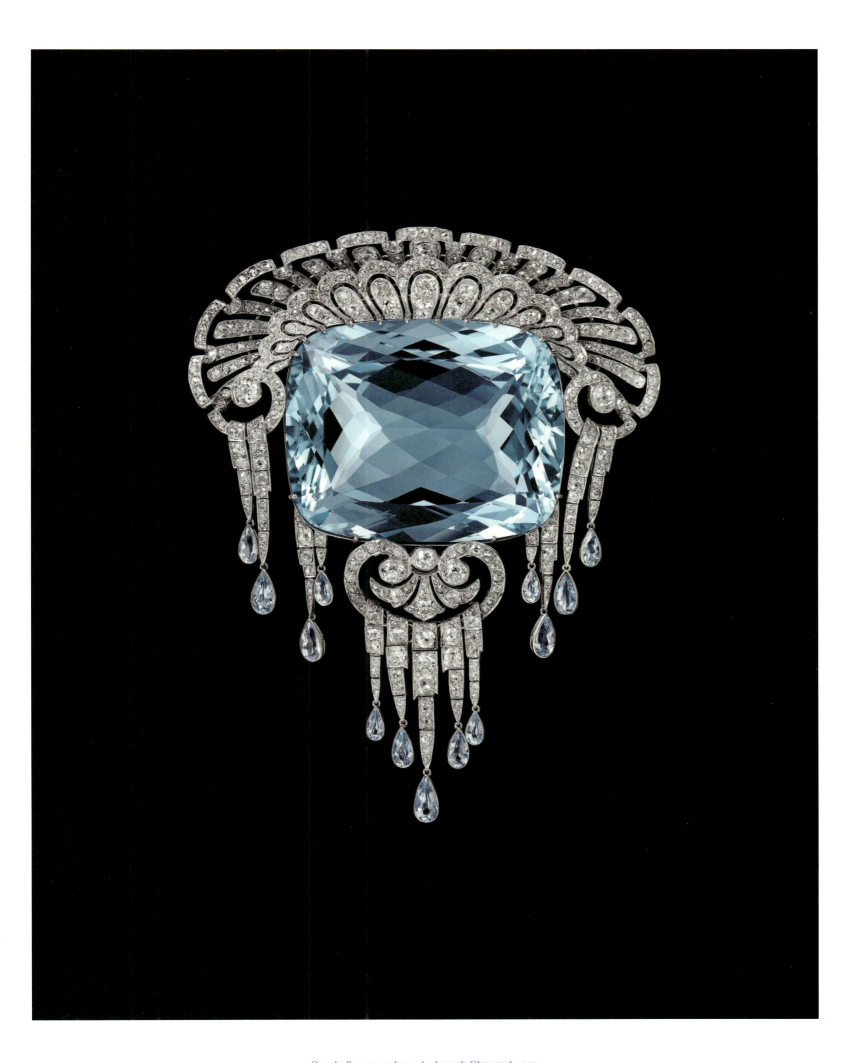

Seashell corsage brooch, Joseph Chaumet, 1913,
gold, silver, diamonds and aquamarine. Private collection.

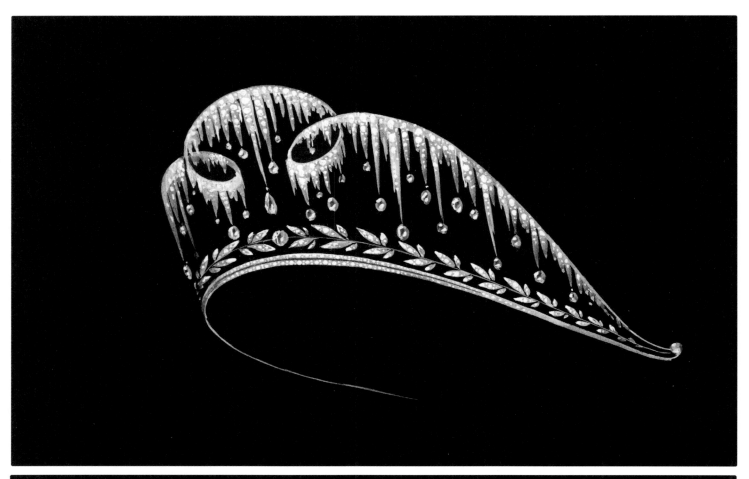

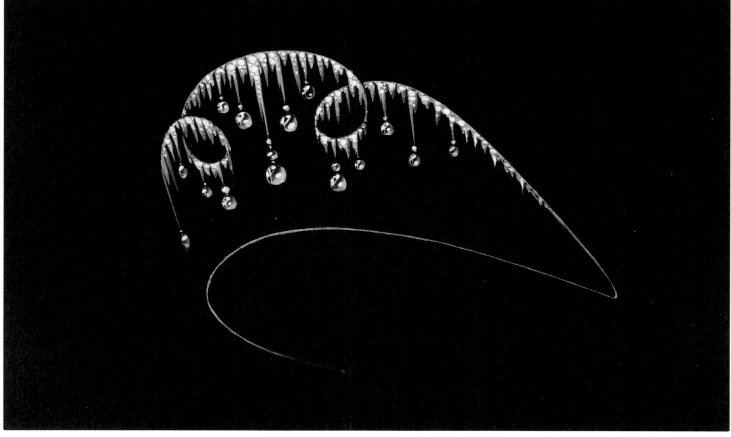

Top Design for a stalactite tiara with foliage bandeau, Joseph Chaumet, drawing studio, c. 1890–1900, graphite pencil, gouache and wash on tinted paper.

Above Design for a tiara with stalactites and water droplets. Joseph Chaumet, drawing studio, c. 1890–1900, graphite pencil, gouache and wash on tinted paper.

Top Design for a rising-sun aigrette,
Joseph Chaumet, drawing studio, 1890–1900,
gouache and wash on translucent paper.

Above Design for a tiara with sunburst motifs,
Joseph Chaumet, drawing studio, *c.* 1890–1900, graphite
pencil, gouache and wash on tinted paper.

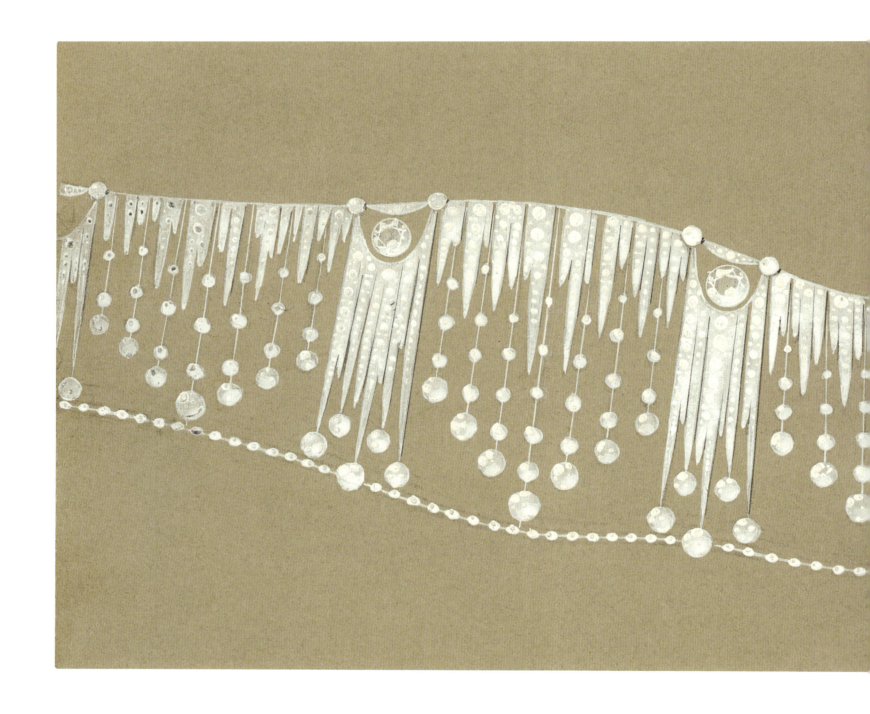

Across the sonorous sky,
In the deepest night,
The radiant stars rain down
The dust of the dawn

Victor Hugo, 'Les étoiles filantes', 1865

Design for a stalactite choker, Joseph Chaumet, drawing studio,
c. 1890–1900, graphite pencil, gouache and wash on tinted paper.

NOTES

The Art of Drawing Jewellery

1 Pablo Picasso, *Propos sur l'art* (Paris: Gallimard, 'Art et Artistes' series, 1998).

2 Numerous craftspeople are involved in the making of a piece of jewellery, including modellers, embossers, drillers, chisellers, engravers, guillochers, enamellers, spray-polishers, gilders, silver-platers, diamond- and stone-cutters and setters.

3 Augustin Duflos, *Recueil de Desseins de Joaillerie, fait par Augustin Duflos, M.d Joaillier à Paris. Et gravé par Claude Duflos* [Paris, c. 1767].

4 Michaël Decrossas, 'Le dessin joaillier' in Bénédicte Gady (ed.), *Le dessin sans réserve: Collections du Musée des Arts Décoratifs*, exhibition catalogue (Paris: Musée des Arts Décoratifs, 2020), p. 224.

5 Gustave Babin, *Une pléiade de maîtres-joailliers 1780–1930* (Paris: Frazier-Soye, 1930), p. 136.

6 Jérôme Neutres, *L'Art du trait* (Paris: Assouline, 2019), pp. 5, 9.

7 Guillaume Glorieux, *Les arts joailliers: Métiers d'excellence* (Paris: Gallimard/L'École des Arts Joailliers, 2019), p. 12.

8 Decrossas, p. 224.

9 Henri Delaborde, *Ingres, sa vie, ses travaux, sa doctrine: D'après les notes manuscrites et les lettres du maître* (Paris: Henri Plon, 1870), p. 123.

10 *Maillechort* is an alloy of copper, nickel and zinc that became extremely popular with French artisans in the first half of the 19th century on account of its ductility, solidity and stability, as well as its sheen, which made it look like silver once it was polished. Joseph Chaumet used nickel-silver to enhance his workshop's creative process. His collection of nickel-silver models comprises just over 700 life-size tiaras, as well as models of necklaces, stomachers and brooches.

11 Babin, pp. 97–98.

12 Babin, pp. 119–20.

13 Ulrich Leben, *L'École royale gratuite de dessin de Paris (1767–1815)* (Saint-Rémy-en-l'Eau: Monelle Hayot, 2004), p. 98.

14 Babin, p. 60.

15 Wibaille's contract from 1903, filed dossier no. 41, Chaumet archives, Paris.

16 'Rapport adressé à Monsieur Chaumet, au sujet des différentes phases traversées par la joaillerie, bijouterie & orfèvrerie depuis quelques années et du parti qu'il y aurait lieu d'en tirer', filed dossier no. 122, Chaumet archives, Paris.

17 1900 Exposition awards, filed dossier no. 12, Chaumet archives, Paris.

18 Chaumet's internal organisation, 'Draughtsmen's department', p. 53, Chaumet archives, Paris.

19 Babin, p. 119.

20 Fabienne Reybaud, *La nature de Chaumet* (Paris: Chaumet/Assouline, 2016), p. 19.

21 Alvar González-Palacios, 'Preface', in Marie-Christine Autin Graz (ed.), *Le bijou dans la peinture* (Paris: Skira/Seuil, 1999), p. 10.

22 Henri Loyrette, 'Ce monde rayonnant de métal et de pierres', in Henri Loyrette (ed.), *Chaumet: Joaillier parisien depuis 1780* (Paris: Flammarion, 2017), p. 27.

Drawing from Nature

1 Alba Cappellieri (ed.), *Van Cleef & Arpels: Temps, Nature, Amour*, exhibition catalogue (Paris, Skira, 2019), p. 192.

2 Fabienne Reybaud, *La nature de Chaumet* (Paris: Chaumet/Assouline, 2016), p. 20.

3 According to age-old aristocratic tradition, such epergnes borrowed the theme of hunting since it was an activity enjoyed by the guests seated around the table, and also referred to the game that they were being served.

4 Alvar González-Palacios, 'Preface', in Marie-Christine Autin Graz (ed.), *Le bijou dans la peinture* (Paris: Skira/Seuil, 1999), p. 12.

5 Letter from Aimé Bonpland, the steward of the Malmaison estate, to Alyre Raffeneau-Delile, 7 March 1814, cited in E. T. Hamy, *Aimé Bonpland, médecin et naturaliste, explorateur de l'Amérique du Sud: Sa vie, son œuvre, sa correspondance* (Paris: Guilmoto, 1906).

6 Reybaud, p. 5.

7 Diana Scarisbrick, 'L'histoire des bijoux dans la peinture (1450–1900)', in Marie-Christine Autin Graz (ed.), *Le bijou dans la peinture* (Paris: Skira/Seuil, 1999), p. 43.

8 Francis Wey, 'Du naturalisme dans l'art, de son principe et de ses conséquences (à propos d'un article de M. Delecluze)', *La Lumière* (30 March 1851), p. 31.

9 Gustave Babin, *Une pléiade de maîtres-joailliers 1780–1930* (Paris: Frazier-Soye, 1930), p. 63.

10 The albums conserved by Chaumet contain numerous references to purchases by the Palais des Tuileries and the 'Château', and in particular a series of 'L.P.' monograms topped with a crown destined for rings, frames, snuffboxes and various other mementoes.

11 Babin, p. 60.

12 This jewel for the head, reflecting the fashion of the 1840s, was named after Marie Mancini, Louis XIV's first love, who sported bouncing ringlets.

13 Babin, p. 77.

14 Diana Scarisbrick, *Chaumet: Joaillier depuis 1780* (Paris: Alain de Gourcuff, 1995), pp. 145–46.

15 Marie-Christine Autin Graz (ed.), *Le bijou dans la peinture* (Paris: Skira/Seuil, 1999), p. 78.

16 Babin, p. 83.

17 He devoted an entire room to pearl jewellery at 12 Place Vendôme.

18 Diana Scarisbrick, *Chaumet: Joaillier depuis 1780*.

19 Babin, pp. 102–9.

20 Laurence Mouillefarine and Évelyne Possémé, *Bijoux Art déco et avant-garde* (Paris: Norma Editions, 2009), p. 10.

21 Ibid.

22 See, for example, Édouard Monod-Herzen, *Principes de morphologie générale*, 2 vols. (Paris: Gauthier-Villars, 1927).

23 Only seven professionals participated in the event: Lacloche, Boucheron, Chaumet, Dusausoy, Mauboussin, Ostertag and Van Cleef & Arpels.

24 A 'clip' was a piece of jewellery that could be attached to a surface thanks to a sprung clasp. The invention of the clip led to the emergence of multi-purpose jewels, heralded by the contemporary press as 'afternoon jewels with a slight air of springtime'. They had the advantage that they could be fixed anywhere: to ears, the lapel of a jacket or the front of a bag.

25 Reybaud, p. 16.

26 *Chaumet en majesté: Joyaux de souveraines depuis 1780*, exhibition catalogue (Paris: Flammarion, 2019), p. 18.

27 Diana Scarisbrick, *Chaumet: Joaillier depuis 1780*, p. 304.

28 *Dess(e)in de nature*, exhibition catalogue (Paris: Chaumet, 2019), p. 54.

Flowers, Trees and Plants, Bestiary, Universe

1 Joséphine Le Foll, *La Peinture de fleurs* (Paris: Hazan, 1997), p. 110.

2 These were groupings of stuffed birds mounted on a miniature tree and covered by a globe, a combination of scientific display and artistic creation.

3 Théophile Gautier, 'Imitation de Byron', in *Poésies complètes* (Paris: George Charpentier, 1889–90).

BIBLIOGRAPHY

Autin Graz, Marie-Christine, *Le bijou dans la peinture*, Paris: Skira / Seuil, 1999

Babin, Gustave, *Une pléiade de maîtres-joailliers, 1780–1930*, Paris: Frazier-Soye, 1930

Boucheron: Free-Spirited Jeweler Since 1858, New York: Harry N. Abrams, 2018

Bourgoing, Catherine de, *Herbier de Joséphine*, Paris: Flammarion, 2019

Décimo, Jean-Michel, *Le goût du dessin*, Paris: Mercure de France, 2020

Glorieux, Guillaume, *Le bijou dessiné*, Paris: Norma Éditions, 2021

Glorieux, Guillaume, *Les arts joailliers: Métiers d'excellence*, Paris: Gallimard / L'École des Arts Joailliers, 2019

Glorieux, Guillaume (ed.), *Paradis d'oiseaux*, Paris: Muséum National d'Histoire Naturelle / MAD / L'École des Arts Joailliers, 2019

Le Foll, Joséphine, *La Peinture de fleurs*, Paris: Hazan, 1997

Loyrette, Henri (ed.), *Chaumet: Joaillier parisien depuis 1780*, Paris: Flammarion, 2017

Mauriès, Patrick, and Évelyne Possémé, *Fauna: The Art of Jewelry*, London: Thames & Hudson, 2017

Mauriès, Patrick, and Évelyne Possémé, *Flora: The Art of Jewelry*, London: Thames & Hudson, 2016

Mouillefarine, Laurence, and Évelyne Possémé, *Art Deco Jewelry*, London: Thames & Hudson, 2009

Neutres, Jérôme, *L'Art du trait*, Paris: Assouline, 2019

Possémé, Évelyne, *Arts et techniques, bijouterie joaillerie*, Paris: Massin Éditeur, 1995

Reybaud, Fabienne, *La nature de Chaumet*, Paris: Chaumet / Éditions Assouline, 2016

Scarisbrick, Diana, *Bijoux de tête, Chaumet de 1804 à nos jours*, Paris: Assouline, 2002

Scarisbrick, Diana, *Chaumet, Master Jewellers since 1780*, Paris: Alain de Gourcuff, 1995

Schneider, Norbert, *Still Life*, Cologne & London: Taschen, 2003

Snowman, A. Kenneth. *Fabergé, Lost and Found: The Recently Discovered Jewelry Designs from the St Petersburg Archives*, New York: Harry N. Abrams, 1993

Vever, Henri, *French Jewelry of the Nineteenth Century (1906–08)*, London: Thames & Hudson, 2001

EXHIBITIONS

'Flower Power', Lille, Musée de l'Hospice Comtesse, Palais des Beaux-Arts, Palais Rameau, Esplanade Euralille, Aéroport de Lille-Lesquin, 6 December 2003–February 2004; catalogue: Dijon: Les Presses du Réel, 2003

'Van Cleef & Arpels: Temps, Nature, Amour', Milan, Palazzo Reale, 30 November 2019– 23 February 2020: catalogue: ed. Alba Cappellieri, Paris: Skira, 2019

'Chaumet en majesté: Joyaux de souveraines depuis 1780', Monaco, Grimaldi Forum, 12 July–29 August 2019; catalogue: Paris: Flammarion, 2019

'Divines joailleries: L'art de Joseph Chaumet (1852–1928)', Paray-le-Monial, Musée du Hiéron, 14 June 2014– 4 January 2015: catalogue: Dominique Dendrael, Diana Scarisbrick and Pierre-Yves Chatagnier, Ville de Paray-le-Monial, 2014

'Brillantes écritures', Paris, Maison Chaumet, 22 February– 1 April 2019: catalogue: Paris: Chaumet, 2019

'Dess(e)in de nature', Paris, Maison Chaumet, 26 July– 7 September 2019: catalogue: Marc Jeanson, Paris: Chaumet, 2019

'Lacloche joailliers, 1892–1967', Paris, L'École des Arts Joailliers, 23 October– 20 December 2019; catalogue: ed. Guillaume Glorieux, Paris: L'École des Arts Joailliers, 2019

'Le dessin sans réserve: Collection du Musée des Arts Décoratifs', Paris, Musée des Arts Décoratifs, 26 March–19 July 2020; catalogue: ed. Bénédicte Gady, Paris: MAD, 2020

'Chaumet et Paris: Deux siècles de création', Paris, Musée Carnavalet, 25 March– 28 June 1998; catalogue: ed. Roselyne Hurel and Diana Scarisbrick, Paris: Paris Musées, 1998

'Le pouvoir des fleurs: Pierre-Joseph Redouté, 1759–1840', Paris, Musée de la Vie Romantique, 25 April– 1 October 2017; catalogue: ed. Catherine de Bourgoing, Sophie Éloy and Jérôme Farigoule, Paris: Paris Musées, 2017

'Bijoux romantiques, 1820–1850: La parure à l'époque de George Sand', Paris, Musée de la Vie Romantique, 3 May– 1 October 2000; catalogue: Paris: Paris Musées, 2000

'Delacroix, Othoniel, Creten: Des fleurs en hiver', Paris, Musée National Eugène-Delacroix, 12 December 2012– 18 March 2013; catalogue: ed. Christophe Leribault, Paris, Louvre Éditions / Le Passage, 2012

'Les gouachés: Un art unique et ignoré', Roubaix, La Piscine–Musée d'Art et d'Industrie André-Diligent, 3 February–1 April 2018: catalogue: Sylvie Botella-Gaudichon and Évelyne Possémé, 2018

'Joséphine: La passion des fleurs et des oiseaux', Rueil-Malmaison, Musée National des Châteaux de Malmaison et Bois-Préau, 2 April–30 June 2014; catalogue: Paris: Artlys, 2014

AUTHOR BIOGRAPHIES

GAËLLE RIO

Chief curator and director of the Musée de la Vie Romantique in Paris, Gaëlle Rio has a doctorate in art history from the Sorbonne. A specialist in the art of the 19th century, she was formerly a curator in the graphic arts department of the Petit Palais, Paris. She has curated many exhibitions and teaches at the École du Louvre and the Institut National du Patrimoine.

MARC JEANSON

Marc Jeanson is a botanist specialising in taxonomy and palms. He has worked at the New York Botanical Garden and the Muséum National d'Histoire Naturelle in Paris and is now botanical director at the Jardin Majorelle in Marrakesh. The many exhibitions he has curated include 'Jardins' at the Grand Palais and 'Végétal' for Maison Chaumet.

ACKNOWLEDGMENTS

The Maison would like to thank its friends Gaëlle Rio and
Marc Jeanson, without whom this book would not have
been possible. It also thanks its collaborators who have
supported the Maison for more than 240 years. This book
is a symbol of the respect due to all of those whose
passion has helped to forge the Maison's reputation.

Thames & Hudson would like to thank Jean-Marc Mansvelt,
Béatrice de Plinval, Claire Gannet, Micahël Lepage, Thibault
Billoir, Raphaël Mingam, Isabelle Vilgrain, Hélène Yvert and
Apolline Descombes, whose invaluable help made this
book a reality.

Gaëlle Rio would like to thank Jean-Marc Mansvelt,
Guillaume Corbel, Béatrice de Plinval, Claire Gannet,
Michaël Lepage, Ehssan Moazen, Sylvie Philippon,
Françoise Roche, Adélia Sabatini, Benoît Verhulle,
Isabelle Vilgrain and Hélène Yvert.

Chaumet, Paris:

Director of publications
Jean-Marc Mansvelt

Editorial director
Isabelle Vilgrain

Senior project editor
Hélène Yvert

Editorial assistant
Apolline Descombes

Thames & Hudson Ltd, London:

Commissioning editor
Adélia Sabatini

Editor and project manager
Flora Spiegel

Production controller
Susanna Ingram

Editor
Sylvie Philippon

Design:

Pierre Péronnet and Wijntje van Rooijen

Translation from the French by Matthew Clarke

On the cover: Necklace with wheat and flower
motifs, drawing studio, c. 1890, Joseph Chaumet
© Chaumet, Paris

First published in the United Kingdom in 2023
by Thames & Hudson Ltd, 181A High Holborn, London
WC1V 7QX

First published in the United States of America in 2023
by Thames & Hudson Inc., 500 Fifth Avenue, New York,
New York 10110

Chaumet: Drawing from Nature
© 2023 Thames & Hudson Ltd, London
Essays and chapter introductions © 2023 Gaëlle Rio
Botanical texts © 2023 Marc Jeanson

All drawings and jewellery pieces are from
the Chaumet collection, Paris.
All historical photographs are from the Chaumet
archives, Paris.

Design by Pierre Péronnet and Wijntje van Rooijen

The jewellery shown in drawings for 2023 collections on
pages 40, 58, 63, 89 and 118 are works in progress and
finished pieces may differ in specification and design.

British Library Cataloguing-in-Publication Data
A catalogue record for this book is available
from the British Library

Library of Congress Control Number: 2023930770

ISBN 978-0-500-02381-5

Printed and bound in China by Artron Art (Group) Co, Ltd.

Printed on FSC-certified papers throughout, with exception
of the cover which is a Japan Green Aid paper

Be the first to know about our new releases,
exclusive content and author events by visiting
thamesandhudson.com
thamesandhudsonusa.com
thamesandhudson.com.au

A sapphire around your neck burns as softly as your tranquil gaze.

Marcel Proust, 'Portraits de peintres et de musiciens',
Les Plaisirs et les Jours, 1896